# THE FUTURE
## OF
# NONFUEL MINERALS

JOHN E. TILTON

# THE FUTURE
# OF
# NONFUEL MINERALS

THE BROOKINGS INSTITUTION
*Washington, D.C.*

Copyright © 1977 by
THE BROOKINGS INSTITUTION
1775 Massachusetts Avenue, N.W., Washington, D.C. 20036

Library of Congress Cataloging in Publication Data:
Tilton, John E
  The future of nonfuel minerals.
  Includes bibliographical references and index.
  1. Mineral industries.   2. Mines and mineral
resources.   I. Title.
HD9506.A2T5      338.2      77-8186
ISBN  0-8157-8460-0

1 2 3 4 5 6 7 8 9

THE BROOKINGS INSTITUTION is an independent organization devoted to nonpartisan research, education, and publication in economics, government, foreign policy, and the social sciences generally. Its principal purposes are to aid in the development of sound public policies and to promote public understanding of issues of national importance.

The Institution was founded on December 8, 1927, to merge the activities of the Institute for Government Research, founded in 1916, the Institute of Economics, founded in 1922, and the Robert Brookings Graduate School of Economics and Government, founded in 1924.

The Board of Trustees is responsible for the general administration of the Institution, while the immediate direction of the policies, program, and staff is vested in the President, assisted by an advisory committee of the officers and staff. The by-laws of the Institution state: "It is the function of the Trustees to make possible the conduct of scientific research, and publication, under the most favorable conditions, and to safeguard the independence of the research staff in the pursuit of their studies and in the publication of the results of such studies. It is not a part of their function to determine, control, or influence the conduct of particular investigations or the conclusions reached."

The President bears final responsibility for the decision to publish a manuscript as a Brookings book. In reaching his judgment on the competence, accuracy, and objectivity of each study, the President is advised by the director of the appropriate research program and weighs the views of a panel of expert outside readers who report to him in confidence on the quality of the work. Publication of a work signifies that it is deemed a competent treatment worthy of public consideration but does not imply endorsement of conclusions or recommendations.

The Institution maintains its position of neutrality on issues of public policy in order to safeguard the intellectual freedom of the staff. Hence interpretations or conclusions in Brookings publications should be understood to be solely those of the authors and should not be attributed to the Institution, to its trustees, officers, or other staff members, or to the organizations that support its research.

# Foreword

UNTIL RECENTLY most nations could easily obtain the mineral commodities needed for industrial production. Multinational mining corporations supplied them reliably, in adequate amounts, and at competitive prices. But the economic and political order is now changing, and relations between suppliers and consumers have been disrupted. More broadly, projections of world population growth and related demands on resources have raised serious questions about the terms of resource availability in the future.

At a meeting in Tokyo in 1974 these problems were addressed by economists from Japan, the European Community, and North America. The meeting was sponsored by the Brookings Institution, the Japan Economic Research Center, and the Kiel Institute for World Economics. This book, which grew out of the author's contribution to that meeting, identifies four possible causes of shortages of nonfuel mineral commodities: depletion of resources, meager expansion of production capacity, erratic demand, and restrictions on trade. In assessing each cause, the author describes the complex and interrelated factors underlying them: the newly won political independence of many mineral producing countries; the volatile and increasingly synchronized business cycles of industrial countries; growing concern about pollution and about the rights of indigenous peoples in mineral-rich areas; and greater reluctance of investors to risk capital in ventures that almost always take years to show profits.

In the author's view, some of the problems may be self-limiting and others susceptible to policy solutions. In the closing chapter he spells out public policies that could eliminate shortages or mitigate their adverse effects.

John E. Tilton, professor of mineral economics at Pennsylvania State University, wrote this book as a member of the Brookings associated staff. He is especially grateful to Edward R. Fried and Henry Owen of Brookings and to Hans H. Landsberg of Resources for the Future for their encouragement and help. Carl E. Beigie, John E. DeYoung, Jr., Alan B. McKerron, George F. Ray, John J. Schanz, Jr., Simon D. Strauss, William A. Vogely, and Jan Zwartendyk made valuable comments on early versions of the manuscript. Elizabeth Semon Bonczar, David A. Hubbard, and Teodoro M. Santos assisted ably in the research. The manuscript was edited by Diane Iredell; Penelope Harpold verified the factual data. The index was prepared by Florence Robinson and the figures were drawn by Clare and Frank Ford.

Financial support for the study was provided by the National Science Foundation. In addition, Resources for the Future, Inc., has for several years supported the author's research on the changing patterns of international metal trade, much of which was useful in this study.

The views expressed here are solely the author's and should not be attributed to the trustees, officers, or other staff members of the Brookings Institution, the National Science Foundation, or Resources for the Future.

BRUCE K. MAC LAURY
*President*

*May 1977*
*Washington, D.C.*

# Contents

## Tables

## Figures

# THE FUTURE
## OF
## NONFUEL MINERALS

CHAPTER ONE

# Introduction

BAUXITE, CHROMITE, TIN, POTASH, IRON, and other nonfuel mineral commodities mined around the world have been, in the past, available to the industrial countries that needed them. Indeed, disruption of their mineral supplies would cripple the economies of the United States, Japan, and Western Europe, although mining and processing, itself, accounts for only a small fraction of their national incomes.

Over the last decade the favorable position of the mineral consuming countries has deteriorated. Chile, Venezuela, Peru, Zaire, Morocco, and other mineral producing countries have taken over operations of multinational mining corporations, once reliable sources of minerals for industrial countries. Canada and Australia, whose investment climates have traditionally favored foreign firms, have increased mineral taxes substantially.

In addition, the specter of producer cartels haunts the industrialized world because of recent experiences: the 1973 oil embargo and subsequent increases in oil prices by the Organization of Petroleum Exporting Countries (OPEC); the formation of new producer associations for copper and other minerals; and unilateral price increases by Jamaica (on bauxite) and Morocco (on phosphate rock).

Sharp price increases and widespread shortages of minerals in 1973 and early 1974, shortly after several studies predicted the early depletion of mineral resources, contributed to the growing concern that, in the future, industrial countries would be unable to obtain the minerals they

1

needed. The price of copper, for example, climbed to $1.51 a pound on the London Metal Exchange in April 1974, a historic high. Shortages of steel and other commodities were so acute during this period that some businessmen resorted to bartering materials.

Later in 1974, the world suffered its worst recession since the 1930s. The demand for minerals fell dramatically, causing prices to plummet and capacity to stand idle. Within a period of eighteen months the price of copper dropped from $1.51 to 54 cents a pound on the London Metal Exchange, even though many producers cut back production by 15 percent or more. While these developments reduced the concern over the adequacy of nonfuel minerals, there are still those who contend that, once the economies of the industrial countries fully recover, shortages will return and perhaps be even more severe than in the past.

This study investigates the future adequacy of nonfuel minerals. Specifically, it attempts to: (1) identify the possible causes of mineral shortages, (2) assess the actual threat they pose for the future, and (3) examine possible public policies that might reduce the likelihood of shortages or alleviate the impact of shortages that do occur.

Before proceeding, however, the concept of a shortage should be clarified. To some, the term implies simply that demand exceeds supply, an imbalance that can always be eliminated by increasing price. This definition is too narrow for public policy purposes, for the solution is one that can cause considerable dislocation and hardship. Thus, this study considers the adequacy of a mineral to be threatened and shortages to exist not only when there are actual physical shortages but also when real prices rise sharply in the short run or persistently in the long run.

Shortages may come about for a number of reasons. The mineral deposits of the world conceivably could become depleted, a prospect examined in the next chapter. Since it takes equipment and facilities to mine and process mineral ores into useful products, shortages could occur if investment in the mineral sector were deficient, a possibility examined in chapters three and four. Even if resources and investment are adequate, temporary shifts in mineral supply or demand from strikes, or fluctuations in the business cycle, or other factors, may create shortages for short periods, as shown in chapter five. Finally, because many nonfuel minerals are produced in areas far from where they are ultimately needed, interruptions or constraints on trade can cause regional shortages; chapter six discusses the potential of producer cartels to impose embargoes and to raise prices. Chapter seven considers economic stockpiling and other public policies that many believe could assure an adequate supply of mineral commodities in the future.

# CHAPTER TWO

# Resource Depletion

CONCERN OVER THE DEPLETION of essential mineral resources is not new. Over sixty years ago, a leader of the American Conservation Movement wrote:

> The five indispensably essential materials in our civilization are wood, water, coal, iron, and agricultural products. . . . We have anthracite coal for but fifty years, and bituminous coal for less than two hundred.
>
> Our supplies of iron ore, mineral oil, and natural gas are being rapidly depleted, and many of the great fields are already exhausted. Mineral resources such as these when once gone are gone forever.[1]

Fear for the adequacy of natural resources can be traced back at least 150 years to the English economist Thomas Malthus.[2]

Though events have stubbornly refused to conform to the pessimistic prophecies of the past, the fear that depletion will seriously constrain future growth and perhaps cause economic collapse has spread widely over the last several years. Many of those most concerned are not ignorant of history and the dismal record of earlier writers. Still, they contend that the world has changed, particularly with regard to the rate at which the human race is consuming mineral resources, making the past a poor guide to the future.

The recent literature contains two views of the depletion problem, one

1. Gifford Pinchot, *The Fight for Conservation* (Doubleday, Page, 1910), p. 123.
2. For a description of some of the early writings on depletion see Harold J. Barnett and Chandler Morse, *Scarcity and Growth* (Johns Hopkins University Press for Resources for the Future, 1963), chaps. 3 and 4.

physical, the other economic. The physical view envisages the world literally running out of mineral deposits. The economic view sees the problem not as the physical exhaustion of all deposits but rather in terms of the higher costs of mineral production that society will have to bear as it depletes its best ore bodies and is forced to turn to lower grade, more remote, and more difficult to exploit deposits. Higher costs will force mineral product prices up, at some point choking off most or all demand. This, of course, could be as devastating in terms of dislocation and hardship and changes in life styles as physical exhaustion would be. This chapter examines and evaluates these two views of depletion.

## The Physical View

The logic of the physical view of depletion is appealingly simple. Since the earth is finite and contains only so much of any substance, the quantity of a particular mineral is physically limited; the total available supply of any mineral is a fixed stock. Demand, on the other hand, is a flow variable; it continues year in and year out. Sooner or later demand has to consume the available supply. According to many versions of the physical view, the end is likely to come sooner rather than later because demand is growing exponentially.[3]

Though it suffers from the shortcomings described later in this chapter, the most prevalent technique for determining the number of years before a mineral resource is exhausted entails estimating the available stock of the mineral and its future production. Most studies of this genre use reserves, or some measure directly related to reserves, to estimate the available supply of minerals.

### Reserve Depletion

Reserves are the minerals in deposits that are known and that can be exploited profitably with existing technology and prices. Current world reserves for all of the major nonfuel mineral commodities, and a number of minor mineral commodities as well, are shown in the first column of table 2-1. The second column shows the average annual mine production

3. Probably the best known example of this position is Donella H. Meadows and others, *The Limits to Growth* (Universe Books, 1972).

Table 2-1. Life Expectancies of World Reserves, Selected Mineral Commodities

| Mineral commodity[a] | 1974 reserves[b] | 1972-74 average annual production[b] | Life expectancy in years, at four growth rates[c] | | | | Average annual production growth, 1947-74 (percent) |
|---|---|---|---|---|---|---|---|
| | | | 0% | 2% | 5% | 10% | |
| Antimony (Sb) | 4.2 × 10^6 | 70.0 × 10^3 | 60 | 40 | 28 | 20 | 2.4 |
| Arsenic (As$_2$O$_3$) | 4.5 × 10^6 | 46.8 × 10^3 | 97 | 54 | 36 | 25 | -0.6 |
| Asbestos | 87.0 × 10^6 | 4.0 × 10^6 | 22 | 18 | 15 | 12 | 6.5 |
| Barite (BaSO$_4$) | 181.4 × 10^6 | 4.3 × 10^6 | 42 | 31 | 23 | 17 | 4.1 |
| Bauxite (ore)[d] | 15.7 × 10^9 | 69.7 × 10^6 | 226 | 86 | 51 | 33 | 9.8 |
| Bismuth (Bi) | 113.4 × 10^3 | 4.2 × 10^3 | 27 | 22 | 18 | 14 | 4.4 |
| Cadmium (Cd) | 1.3 × 10^6 | 17.0 × 10^3 | 74 | 46 | 32 | 22 | 4.7 |
| Chromium (ore) | 1.7 × 10^9 | 6.5 × 10^6 | 263 | 93 | 54 | 35 | 5.3 |
| Cobalt (Co) | 2.4 × 10^6 | 25.3 × 10^3 | 97 | 54 | 36 | 25 | 5.8 |
| Copper (Cu) | 390.0 × 10^6 | 7.0 × 10^6 | 56 | 38 | 27 | 20 | 4.8 |
| Diamond (industrial) | 680.0 × 10^6 | 31.4 × 10^6 | 22 | 18 | 15 | 12 | 5.4 |
| Fluorspar (90% CaF$_2$) | 106.1 × 10^6 | 4.5 × 10^6 | 23 | 19 | 16 | 13 | 7.5 |
| Gold (Au) | 4.0 × 10^4 | 1.3 × 10^3 | 30 | 24 | 19 | 15 | 2.4 |
| Ilmenite (conc.)[e] | 516.9 × 10^6 | 3.4 × 10^6 | 150 | 70 | 44 | 29 | 9.5 |
| Iron (Fe) | 87.7 × 10^9 | 0.5 × 10^9 | 167 | 74 | 46 | 30 | 7.0 |
| Lead (Pb) | 145.1 × 10^6 | 3.5 × 10^6 | 42 | 31 | 23 | 17 | 3.8 |
| Magnesium (Mg)[f] | ... | 5.1 × 10^6 | .. | .. | .. | .. | 7.7 |
| Manganese (Mn)[g] | 1.9 × 10^9 | 10.1 × 10^6 | 190 | 79 | 48 | 31 | 6.5 |
| Mercury (Hg) | 182.3 × 10^3 | 9.4 × 10^3 | 19 | 17 | 14 | 11 | 2.0 |
| Molybdenum (Mo) | 5.0 × 10^6 | 71.6 × 10^3 | 70 | 44 | 31 | 22 | 7.3 |
| Nickel (Ni) | 44.4 × 10^6 | 0.7 × 10^6 | 67 | 43 | 30 | 22 | 6.9 |

| | | | | | | | |
|---|---|---|---|---|---|---|---|
| Phosphate rock | $13.0 \times 10^9$ | $99.4 \times 10^6$ | 128 | 64 | 41 | 28 | 7.3 |
| Platinum group (metal) | $1.9 \times 10^4$ | $0.2 \times 10^3$ | 117 | 61 | 39 | 27 | 9.7 |
| Potash ($K_2O$) | $80.7 \times 10^9$ | $22.2 \times 10^6$ | 3,638 | 217 | 107 | 62 | 9.0 |
| Silver (Ag) | $1.9 \times 10^5$ | $9.3 \times 10^3$ | 20 | 17 | 14 | 12 | 2.2 |
| Sulfur (S) | $2.0 \times 10^9$ | $46.8 \times 10^6$ | 44 | 32 | 24 | 18 | 6.7 |
| Tin (Sn) | $9.9 \times 10^6$ | $0.2 \times 10^6$ | 42 | 31 | 23 | 17 | 2.7 |
| Tungsten (W) | $1.6 \times 10^6$ | $39.0 \times 10^3$ | 42 | 31 | 23 | 17 | 3.8 |
| Vanadium (V)[h] | $9.7 \times 10^6$ | $15.7 \times 10^3$ | 462 | 131 | 71 | 43 | 11.1 |
| Zinc (Zn) | $118.8 \times 10^6$ | $5.6 \times 10^6$ | 21 | 18 | 15 | 12 | 4.7 |

Sources: U.S. Bureau of Mines, *Commodity Data Summaries 1972* (U.S. Bureau of Mines, 1972), and ibid. *1973, 1974, 1975, 1976*; Donald A. Brobst and Walden P. Pratt, eds., *United States Mineral Resources*, Geological Survey professional paper 820 (GPO, 1973); U.S. Bureau of Mines, *Minerals Yearbook 1948*, and ibid. *1974* (GPO, 1950 and 1976).

a. The notation in parentheses following the name of a mineral commodity indicates what the reserve and production figures actually measure. For example, for copper they measure contained metal (Cu), for ilmenite they measure concentrates (conc.), and for bauxite and chromium they measure ore (ore).
b. Measured in metric tons except for diamonds, which are measured in carats.
c. Life expectancy figures were calculated before reserve and average annual production data were rounded.
d. Figures include only those ores that contain 52 percent or more aluminum.
e. Figures are for noncommunist countries only.
f. Production figure is based on 1973 and 1974 data. There are vast reserves of magnesium, and life expectancies would measure in centuries.
g. Concentrate is assumed to contain 46 percent manganese for the production figure and 35 percent for the reserve figure.
h. Production figure is based on 1972 and 1973 data and includes the output of only noncommunist countries

for these mineral products over the 1972–74 period. The next four columns reveal the number of years current reserves would last if future production grew at the annual rate of 0, 2, 5, and 10 percent. The actual growth rates over the postwar period are given in the last column, for comparison purposes.

As one would expect, reserve life expectancies vary greatly depending on the mineral commodity. Reserves of magnesium, which can be recovered economically from seawater, are abundant. Similarly, potash reserves would last several millenia at current rates of production. However, for many other nonfuel mineral products, such as bauxite, copper, iron, manganese, nickel, and phosphate rock, reserve life expectancies vary between 50 and 250 years. At the lower end of the spectrum, the reserves of mercury are not sufficient for even 20 years at current rates of production. If consumption and production grow in the future, as they almost certainly will, the reserve life of mineral commodities is significantly shortened, particularly for those with relatively large reserves.

At first blush, these findings are disconcerting. Indeed, on the basis of such data, some have argued that mankind has at best several centuries and perhaps as little as several decades before the mineral base of its industrial society is gone. Fortunately, this conclusion is misleading and most likely wrong, largely because reserves are a poor measure of the available stock of mineral commodities.

By definition, reserves cover only those minerals contained in deposits that are known and that can be exploited profitably with existing technology and prices. Thus, reserves constitute only a subset, and typically an extremely small subset, of the resource base, the total amount of a mineral contained in the earth's crust. There are two reasons for this: first, a number of ore bodies have yet to be discovered; and second, with existing technology and prices, many deposits are not economical to exploit because of remote locations, low ore grade, or other factors.

While the resource base for any particular mineral commodity is a fixed stock, its reserves are not. Reserves of iron and copper, for example, have increased greatly over the postwar period (see figure 2-1). Indeed, world production would have completely consumed copper reserves by the early 1970s had no new reserves been found. However, additions to reserves more than offset production, so that copper reserves today are far larger than in the early postwar period.

As for iron, after World War II many feared that the world faced a

Figure 2-1.  *World Reserves of Contained Iron and Copper, 1946–75, and Effect of Cumulative Production on 1946 Reserves*

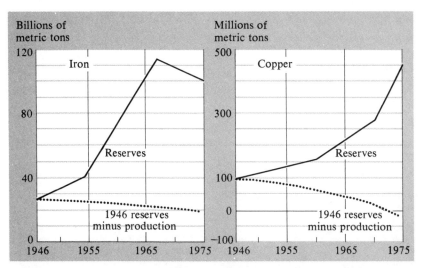

Sources: Production figures, United Nations, *Statistical Yearbook 1955* (Statistical Office of the United Nations, Department of Economic and Social Affairs), ibid. *1965, 1975*; reserve figures, UN Department of Economic Affairs, *Proceedings of the United Nations Scientific Conference on the Conservation and Utilization of Resources,* vol. 2 (1951), p. 2 for iron and copper in 1946; UN, Department of Economic and Social Affairs, *Survey of World Iron Ore Resources* (1970), p. 8 for iron in 1954 and 1967; U.S. Bureau of Mines, *Mineral Facts and Problems* (GPO, 1960), p. 250 for copper in 1960; U.S. Bureau of Mines, *Commodity Data Summaries 1976* (USBM, January 1976), pp. 47 and 83 for copper and iron in 1975.

serious shortage of this important mineral product, for wartime consumption had depleted the rich deposits of the Mesabi Range in northern Minnesota. Since then, major new deposits have been found in Canada, Brazil, Venezuela, Liberia, Australia, and other countries; and new technology has made the taconite deposits in northern Minnesota and elsewhere viable sources of iron ore. These developments have added billions of tons to reserves.

Moreover, copper and iron are not unusual in this respect. New discoveries and technology add to the reserves of many minerals at a rate that exceeds depletion. As a result, reserves of nearly all mineral commodities are larger today than in the early postwar period (see table 2-2).

*Resource Base Depletion*

Reserves or some multiple of reserves are weak measures of the total available supply of a mineral, suggesting that a stronger measure might be

Table 2-2. *Cumulative Production and Additions to World Reserves,*
*Selected Mineral Commodities, 1950–74*

Metric tons unless otherwise stated

| Mineral commodity | 1950 reserves | 1974 reserves | 1950-74 cumulative production | 1950-74 addition to reserves[a] | Addition to reserves as a percentage of 1950 reserves[b] |
|---|---|---|---|---|---|
| Antimony | $3.5 \times 10^6$ | $4.2 \times 10^6$ | $1.5 \times 10^6$ | $2.2 \times 10^6$ | 64 |
| Asbestos | $3.9 \times 10^7$ | $8.7 \times 10^7$ | $6.2 \times 10^7$ | $1.1 \times 10^8$ | 281 |
| Bauxite | $1.4 \times 10^9$ | $1.6 \times 10^{10}$ | $8.5 \times 10^8$ | $1.5 \times 10^{10}$ | 1,103 |
| Chromium | $1.0 \times 10^8$ | $1.7 \times 10^9$ | $9.6 \times 10^7$ | $1.7 \times 10^9$ | 1,696 |
| Cobalt | $7.9 \times 10^5$ | $2.4 \times 10^6$ | $4.4 \times 10^5$ | $2.0 \times 10^6$ | 258 |
| Copper | $1.0 \times 10^8$ | $3.9 \times 10^8$ | $1.1 \times 10^8$ | $4.0 \times 10^8$ | 403 |
| Diamond[c] | $5.8 \times 10^8$ | $6.8 \times 10^8$ | $8.2 \times 10^8$ | $9.3 \times 10^8$ | 160 |
| Fluorspar | $2.2 \times 10^7$ | $1.1 \times 10^8$ | $6.5 \times 10^7$ | $1.5 \times 10^8$ | 696 |
| Gold | $3.1 \times 10^4$ | $4.0 \times 10^4$ | $2.9 \times 10^4$ | $3.7 \times 10^4$ | 122 |
| Iron | $1.9 \times 10^{10}$ | $8.8 \times 10^{10}$ | $7.3 \times 10^9$ | $7.6 \times 10^{10}$ | 401 |
| Lead | $4.0 \times 10^7$ | $1.5 \times 10^8$ | $6.3 \times 10^7$ | $1.7 \times 10^8$ | 433 |
| Manganese | $5.0 \times 10^8$ | $1.9 \times 10^9$ | $1.6 \times 10^8$ | $1.6 \times 10^9$ | 313 |
| Mercury[d] | $1.3 \times 10^5$ | $1.8 \times 10^5$ | $1.9 \times 10^5$ | $2.5 \times 10^5$ | 188 |
| Molybdenum[e] | $4.0 \times 10^6$ | $5.0 \times 10^6$ | $1.1 \times 10^6$ | $2.0 \times 10^6$ | 51 |
| Nickel[e] | $1.4 \times 10^7$ | $4.4 \times 10^7$ | $9.4 \times 10^6$ | $3.9 \times 10^7$ | 281 |
| Phosphate rock | $2.6 \times 10^9$ | $1.3 \times 10^{10}$ | $1.3 \times 10^9$ | $1.2 \times 10^{10}$ | 450 |
| Platinum group | $7.8 \times 10^2$ | $1.9 \times 10^4$ | $1.7 \times 10^3$ | $2.0 \times 10^4$ | 2,564 |
| Potash | $5.0 \times 10^9$ | $8.1 \times 10^{10}$ | $3.0 \times 10^8$ | $7.6 \times 10^{10}$ | 1,525 |
| Silver | $1.6 \times 10^5$ | $1.9 \times 10^5$ | $2.0 \times 10^5$ | $2.3 \times 10^5$ | 141 |
| Sulfur | $4.0 \times 10^8$ | $2.0 \times 10^9$ | $6.1 \times 10^8$ | $2.2 \times 10^9$ | 554 |
| Tin | $6.0 \times 10^6$ | $1.0 \times 10^7$ | $4.6 \times 10^6$ | $8.6 \times 10^6$ | 144 |
| Tungsten | $2.4 \times 10^6$ | $1.6 \times 10^6$ | $7.6 \times 10^5$ | $-4.3 \times 10^4$ | $-1.8$ |
| Zinc | $7.0 \times 10^7$ | $1.2 \times 10^8$ | $9.7 \times 10^7$ | $1.5 \times 10^8$ | 210 |

Sources: Reserve figures are based on information found in United Nations, Department of Economic Affairs, *Proceedings of the United Nations Scientific Conference on the Conservation and Utilization of Resources* vol. 2, E/Conf. 7/7 (1951), p. 2; U.S. President's Materials Policy Commission, *Resources for Freedom*, vol. 2 (GPO, 1952); U.S. Bureau of Mines, *Mineral Facts and Problems* (GPO, 1956); U.S. Bureau of Mines, *Commodity Data Summaries 1975* (GPO, 1975). Cumulative production figures are calculated from United Nations, *Statistical Yearbook* (1950–76).

a. Derived by adding 1950–74 cumulative production to 1974 reserves and subtracting 1950 reserves.
b. Calculated before reserve and cumulative production data were rounded.
c. Measured in carats.
d. Reserve figure for 1950 is incomplete for communist countries.
e. Reserve figure for 1950 excludes communist countries.

the mineral's resource base. The latter, by definition, encompasses all of the material found in the earth's crust and so does not change with new discoveries, technological progress, or fluctuations in prices.

Figures on the resource base for a number of nonfuel mineral commodities are shown in table 2-3 along with their life expectancies under various assumptions of growth in production. The resource base for all of the mineral commodities identified would sustain production at current rates for millions, in many cases billions, of years. Thus, if the resource base is used as a measure of mineral availability and if production of mineral products in the future is sustained at current levels, the physical depletion of minerals becomes a remote and unpressing problem.

However, the table also reveals that even moderate rates of growth in production greatly shorten the number of years the resource base will last. For example, at an annual growth rate of 5 percent, the life expectancy of the resource base drops from millions and billions of years to under 600 years, a dramatic illustration of the effects of exponential growth.

There are, however, serious problems associated with looking at depletion in this way. First, aside from a few minor exceptions, such as the fissioning of uranium, elemental minerals are never destroyed or transmuted. Even if all of the copper resource base, for example, were consumed, the copper produced in the process would be available for recycling and reuse. In some instances it might be in a form that entails high costs to recover and upgrade, but the stock of available copper would not have decreased. A more serious problem inherent in this view of depletion is that long before the resource base for the mineral is consumed, extraction and processing costs would rise to such high levels that demand would be stifled. This leads one to the economic view of depletion.

## The Economic View

The economic view of depletion anticipates that the real costs of finding and processing minerals will rise as producers are forced to turn to poorer deposits and that eventually this will force society to curtail its consumption of mineral products. Proponents of this view tend to fall into two groups. In the first group are those who believe that depletion will increase the energy, labor, capital, and other inputs required per unit of output and so will raise the cost incurred by producers. Those in the second group are not as concerned about the rise in private costs of mineral products, nor are all of them certain these costs will rise.[4] Instead, they are disturbed about the social costs as producers turn to lower grade and more remote deposits. Wastes and pollutants discarded into the air, water, and soil increase with resource production and consumption. As grade of ore falls, more and more land must be disturbed to recover a given amount of a mineral commodity. More energy is used, contributing to pollution and land use problems. In addition, the development of remote deposits in isolated areas may alter or destroy the way of life of the natives. The Eskimo

4. See, for example, David B. Brooks and P. W. Andrews, "Mineral Resources, Economic Growth, and World Population," *Science* (July 5, 1974), pp. 13–19.

Table 2-3. Life Expectancies of Resource Bases, Selected Mineral Commodities

| Mineral commodity | Resource base[a] (metric tons) | 1972–74 average annual production (metric tons) | Life expectancy in years, at four growth rates[b] | | | | Average annual production growth, 1947–74 (percent) |
|---|---|---|---|---|---|---|---|
| | | | 0% | 2% | 5% | 10% | |
| Aluminum | $2.0 \times 10^{18}$ | $12.0 \times 10^{6}$ | $166.0 \times 10^{9}$ | 1,107 | 468 | 247 | 9.8 |
| Antimony | $14.9 \times 10^{12}$ | $70.0 \times 10^{3}$ | $214.0 \times 10^{6}$ | 771 | 332 | 177 | 2.4 |
| Arsenic[c] | $52.8 \times 10^{12}$ | $35.5 \times 10^{3}$ | $1.5 \times 10^{9}$ | 869 | 372 | 197 | –0.6 |
| Barium[d] | $9.4 \times 10^{15}$ | $2.4 \times 10^{6}$ | $4.0 \times 10^{9}$ | 918 | 392 | 208 | 4.1 |
| Bismuth | $0.1 \times 10^{12}$ | $4.2 \times 10^{3}$ | $24.0 \times 10^{6}$ | 661 | 287 | 154 | 4.4 |
| Cadmium | $3.6 \times 10^{12}$ | $17.0 \times 10^{3}$ | $210.5 \times 10^{6}$ | 771 | 332 | 177 | 4.7 |
| Chromium[e] | $2.6 \times 10^{15}$ | $2.1 \times 10^{6}$ | $1.3 \times 10^{9}$ | 861 | 368 | 196 | 5.3 |
| Cobalt | $600.0 \times 10^{12}$ | $25.3 \times 10^{3}$ | $23.8 \times 10^{9}$ | 1,009 | 428 | 227 | 5.8 |
| Copper | $1.5 \times 10^{15}$ | $7.0 \times 10^{6}$ | $216.0 \times 10^{6}$ | 772 | 332 | 177 | 4.8 |
| Flourine[f] | $10.8 \times 10^{15}$ | $2.0 \times 10^{6}$ | $5.4 \times 10^{9}$ | 934 | 398 | 211 | 7.5 |
| Gold | $84.0 \times 10^{9}$ | $1.3 \times 10^{3}$ | $62.8 \times 10^{6}$ | 709 | 307 | 164 | 2.4 |
| Iron | $1.4 \times 10^{18}$ | $0.5 \times 10^{9}$ | $2.6 \times 10^{9}$ | 898 | 383 | 203 | 7.0 |
| Lead | $290.0 \times 10^{12}$ | $3.5 \times 10^{6}$ | $83.5 \times 10^{6}$ | 724 | 313 | 167 | 3.8 |
| Magnesium[c] | $672.0 \times 10^{15}$ | $5.1 \times 10^{6}$ | $131.5 \times 10^{9}$ | 1,095 | 463 | 244 | 7.7 |
| Manganese[g] | $31.2 \times 10^{15}$ | $10.1 \times 10^{6}$ | $3.1 \times 10^{9}$ | 906 | 386 | 205 | 6.5 |
| Mercury | $2.1 \times 10^{12}$ | $9.4 \times 10^{3}$ | $223.5 \times 10^{6}$ | 773 | 333 | 178 | 2.0 |
| Molybdenum | $31.2 \times 10^{12}$ | $71.6 \times 10^{3}$ | $436.0 \times 10^{6}$ | 807 | 346 | 185 | 7.3 |
| Nickel | $2.1 \times 10^{12}$ | $0.7 \times 10^{6}$ | $3.2 \times 10^{6}$ | 559 | 246 | 133 | 6.9 |
| Phosphorus[h] | $28.8 \times 10^{15}$ | $15.2 \times 10^{6}$ | $1.9 \times 10^{9}$ | 881 | 376 | 200 | 7.3 |
| Potassium[c] | $408.0 \times 10^{15}$ | $18.4 \times 10^{6}$ | $22.1 \times 10^{9}$ | 1,005 | 427 | 226 | 9.0 |
| Platinum | $1.1 \times 10^{12}$ | $0.2 \times 10^{3}$ | $6.7 \times 10^{9}$ | 944 | 402 | 213 | 9.7 |

| | | | | | | | |
|---|---|---|---|---|---|---|---|
| Silver | $1.8 \times 10^{12}$ | $9.3 \times 10^{3}$ | $194.2 \times 10^{6}$ | 766 | 330 | 176 | 2.2 |
| Sulfur[c] | $9.6 \times 10^{15}$ | $46.8 \times 10^{6}$ | $205.3 \times 10^{6}$ | 769 | 331 | 177 | 6.7 |
| Tin | $40.8 \times 10^{12}$ | $0.2 \times 10^{6}$ | $172.2 \times 10^{6}$ | 760 | 327 | 175 | 2.7 |
| Titanium[i] | $153.6 \times 10^{15}$ | $1.2 \times 10^{6}$ | $124.0 \times 10^{9}$ | 1,092 | 462 | 244 | 9.5 |
| Tungsten | $26.4 \times 10^{12}$ | $39.0 \times 10^{3}$ | $677.2 \times 10^{6}$ | 829 | 355 | 189 | 3.8 |
| Vanadium | $3.4 \times 10^{15}$ | $15.7 \times 10^{3}$ | $213.8 \times 10^{9}$ | 1,120 | 473 | 250 | 11.1 |
| Zinc | $2.2 \times 10^{15}$ | $5.6 \times 10^{3}$ | $398.6 \times 10^{9}$ | 1,151 | 486 | 256 | 4.7 |

Sources: The data on the resource base are based on information in Brobst and Pratt, eds., *United States Mineral Resources*, Geological Survey professional paper 820 (GPO, 1973); pp. 22–23; Tan Lee and Chi-Lung Yao, "Abundance of Chemical Elements in the Earth's Crust and Its Major Tectonic Units," *International Geology Review* (July 1970), pp. 778–86. The figures for the 1972–74 average annual production and the annual percentage growth in production for 1947–74 are from table 2-1 and the sources cited there.

a. The resource base for a mineral commodity is calculated by multiplying its elemental abundance measured in grams per metric ton times the total weight (24 × 10^18) in metric tons of the earth's crust. It reflects the quantity of that material found in the earth's crust.

b. Life expectancy figures were calculated before resource base and average annual production data were rounded.

c. Amount in the earth's crust was calculated from data in Lee and Yao.

d. Production figure assumes that concentrates are 94 percent BaSO₄.

e. Production figure assumes that concentrates are 46 percent chromium.

f. Production figure assumes that concentrates are 90 percent CaF₂.

g. Production figure assumes that concentrates are 46 percent manganese.

h. Production figure assumes that concentrates are 35 percent P₂O₅.

i. Production figure assumes that ilmenite concentrates are 60 percent TiO₂.

culture of Alaska and northern Canada may suffer this fate in the near future.

Whether the private and social costs of mineral production will rise appreciably in the future is an open question. While the depletion of high-grade, easy-to-find, and readily accessible deposits pushes costs up over time, improvements in technology have the opposite effect and historically have overwhelmed the cost-increasing effect of depletion, causing real costs to fall.[5] For example, Barnett and Morse found that from 1870 to 1957 the index (1929=100) of labor-capital input per unit of mineral output fell from 210 to 47 in the United States.[6] Although they did not take into account pollution and other social costs, it is unlikely that these costs increased so greatly over this period as to offset the substantial decline in private costs.

Technology achieved this reduction in costs in a variety of ways. Over the last century, exploration has been revolutionized. In the 1870s most mineral deposits were found by lone prospectors, who depended on surface features of the land and in most cases actual outcrops of ore. Today, exploration teams rely on geophysical and geochemical knowledge unknown a hundred years ago. They use magnetometers, gravimeters, and Geiger counters, as well as modern photographic techniques (some relying on earth satellites) to locate deposits buried under perhaps hundreds of feet of overburden. Airplanes permit aerial surveys and extend the mobility and working season of exploration geologists. Helicopters are used in geochemical sampling, and computers aid in analyzing exploration data.

Similarly, great progress has been made in the processing, transportation, and utilization of mineral products. Larger shovels, bigger trucks, and other improvements in earth moving equipment have substantially reduced costs. New processing technologies have made possible the winning of metals from previously intractable ores, as the increasing amounts of iron from taconite and of nickel from laterite ore demonstrate. Larger vessels and more efficient loading and unloading facilities have revolutionized the ocean transportation of bulk commodities and made the exploitation of remote mineral deposits economical.[7]

5. There are other factors that may also reduce costs, such as the discovery of new high-grade deposits or the increasing realization of scale economies, but their impact over the long run is small compared to that of technological change.
6. Barnett and Morse, *Scarcity and Growth*, p. 8.
7. For a more detailed discussion of the impact of technological change on the

Technology has further lessened the impact of depletion on costs by reducing the demand for mineral products. Electrolytic plating, for example, has substantially diminished the amount of tin required to make a tin can. New materials produced from relatively abundant minerals have been developed and used in place of older, scarcer materials, for example, the substitution of plastic for copper piping, aluminum for tin cans, and synthetic for natural rubber. In addition to material substitution, technology has promoted functional substitution, which entails a completely different method of accomplishing an end. The use of telephone communications instead of travel, frozen foods instead of canned goods, electronic pocket calculators instead of mechanical adding machines are but a few examples. Such substitutions have changed, and often reduced, the materials needed to perform certain jobs.[8]

But all of this is history. Is there any guarantee that technological progress will continue to offset the cost-increasing tendencies of depletion? In addressing this question, it is useful to divide the future into the near term (the next twenty-five years) and the long term (the twenty-first century and beyond).

*The Next Twenty-five Years*

Some idea of the impact of depletion on costs over the rest of this century can be gained by looking at the reserve life expectancies shown in table 2-1. Since reserves include only those deposits that are identified and profitable to exploit with present technology and prices, depletion should not dictate increases in costs for those mineral products whose reserve life expectancies exceed twenty-five years.[9] There are, however, pitfalls in this

---

transportation of minerals, particularly iron ore, see Gerald Manners, *The Changing World Market for Iron Ore, 1950–1980* (Johns Hopkins University Press for Resources for the Future, 1971), chaps. 9 and 10.

8. For an interesting description of the potential of electronics to effect widespread functional substitution, and the implications for mineral use, see A. G. Chynoweth, "Electronic Materials: Functional Substitutions," *Science* (February 20, 1976), pp. 725–32.

9. If the reserves of a mineral are concentrated in mines producing at optimal scale, depletion could conceivably cause production costs to rise before the end of the century even though the life expectancy of reserves exceeded twenty-five years. For example, suppose that two mines possessed all of the reserves and accounted for all of the production of a particular mineral, that they had the same annual output, and that the reserves of one were ten times annual production while the reserves of

type of exercise, for reliable estimates of the life expectancies of world reserves require accurate estimates of (1) mineral consumption, (2) the recycling or secondary production of mineral products, and (3) mineral reserves.

Projections of consumption depend crucially on what assumptions the forecaster makes regarding population growth and the intensity of per capita mineral use. Predicting the latter is particularly difficult. In the past, many have simply assumed that mineral consumption would continue to grow in some fixed proportion to income. Recently, however, this assumption has been challenged by the intensity-of-use hypothesis, which contends that mineral consumption increases first at an increasing rate and then at a decreasing rate as per capita income rises. Simple correlations between per capita income and the consumption of certain mineral commodities appear to follow this pattern.[10]

The major reason for this tendency, however, is not entirely clear. To some extent, the tendency may reflect changes in the composition of de-

the other were fifty times annual production. Although the life expectancy of reserves at current production levels for this mineral averages thirty years, production costs could rise after the depletion of the first mine in ten years. To maintain annual production after that time might require either that the second mine expand its annual production beyond the optimal level or that new mines be developed to exploit higher-cost deposits not now considered as reserves. For more on this and other deficiencies of mineral life expectancies see Jan Zwartendyk, "The Life Index of Mineral Reserves—A Statistical Mirage," *The Canadian Mining and Metallurgical Bulletin,* vol. 67, no. 750 (October 1974), pp. 67–70.

Moreover, it should be noted that even if depletion does not cause a rise in the production costs of mineral products with twenty-five years of reserves, their prices could still increase before the end of the century unless adequate additions to reserves are made, for the market tends to increase the value of those resources that appear to be growing scarce, assuring their optimal use over time. This function of the market is described in the literature on the theory of exhaustion. See, for example, Harold Hotelling, "The Economics of Exhaustible Resources," *Journal of Political Economy,* vol. 39, no. 2 (April 1931), pp. 137–75; Richard L. Gordon, "A Reinterpretation of the Pure Theory of Exhaustion," *Journal of Political Economy,* vol. 75, no. 3 (June 1967), pp. 274–86; and Robert M. Solow, "The Economics of Resources or the Resources of Economics," *American Economic Review* (May 1974), pp. 1–14.

10. See Committee on Economic Studies, *Projection 85: World Steel Demand* (Brussels: International Iron and Steel Institute, 1972); Wilfred Malenbaum, *Material Requirements in the United States and Abroad in the Year 2000,* a research project prepared for the National Commission on Materials Policy; Wilfred Malenbaum, "Laws of Demand for Minerals," *Proceedings of the Council of Economics* (American Institute of Mining, Metallurgical, and Petroleum Engineers, 1975), pp. 147–53; and Brooks and Andrews, "Mineral Resources, Economic Growth, and World Population."

mand that occur as per capita income rises. In the early stages of development, countries tend to concentrate on building basic industries and infrastructure, such as roads, railroads, ports, power plants, and schools. At some point, as income continues to rise, demand begins to shift toward services, which may be less material intensive.[11]

There is, however, another possible explanation for changes in intensity of use, which may be more important than the evolution in demand that occurs with development. Mineral commodities like other products tend to go through life cycles. When they are relatively new, improvements in technology come quickly, reducing their costs and enhancing their physical attributes. During this stage, they capture markets from competing materials and grow faster than the economy as a whole. With time, the favorable impact that technological change has on both cost and quality tends to abate, and other new materials are introduced. As the latter penetrate existing markets, mineral commodities introduced earlier are likely to experience a decline in use per unit of income. This explanation implies that changes in the intensity of use of minerals depend primarily on time, rather than on changes in per capita income.[12]

Whatever the reasons for this phenomenon, changes in intensity of use greatly increase the difficulty of projecting future mineral consumption. Still, consumption is unlikely to grow at an annual rate of more than 10 percent or less than 0 percent over the remainder of this century. Thus, reserve life expectancies are calculated in table 2-1 on the assumption that future mineral production will grow at 0, 2, 5, or 10 percent a year. While this spectrum appears to be reasonable for most minerals, a rapid increase in secondary production may prevent the primary production of some minerals from growing as rapidly as consumption.

Secondary production entails collecting, sorting, transporting, and processing scrap, either new scrap generated in the manufacturing process or old scrap recovered from finished products that have been used and discarded. For new scrap, these steps are inexpensive to perform compared to the cost of primary production, and consequently most new scrap is

---

11. Some services, however, are material intensive, such as government expenditures for military equipment. This has led some to question whether services, on balance, actually are less material intensive. See William A. Vogely, "Is There a Law of Demand for Minerals?" *Earth and Mineral Sciences,* vol. 45, no. 7 (April 1976), pp. 49, 52, and 53.

12. Some empirical support for this is found in ibid., p. 52.

recycled. For old scrap, recycling costs vary greatly depending on the end use. The lead in automobile batteries, for example, is cheap to recover and reprocess, but just the opposite is true for the lead in gasoline and paint. As a result, as the level of secondary production rises, scrap must be recovered from increasingly difficult and expensive sources. This causes secondary costs to rise, and eventually they approach infinity either because the collection costs become prohibitively high, as in the case of lead in gasoline, or because the stock of available scrap is exhausted.

The incentive to expand secondary output continues up to the point where its costs just equal the costs of primary production. Thus, secondary output should increase for those mineral commodities whose primary costs are rising relative to secondary costs (at current output levels).[13] Three recent developments tend to raise the relative costs of primary production. (1) The cost of abiding by increasingly restrictive environmental regulations generally is higher for primary producers. (2) Primary production tends to use more energy per unit of output than secondary production and so has been hurt more by the recent increases in energy prices. (3) Royalty charges and taxes on primary producers have increased sharply in many countries, particularly those with high-grade deposits, as governments try to capture a larger share of the revenue generated by their domestic mineral operations. It is too soon to tell the actual amount secondary output will increase because of these factors; it is likely to vary from one mineral to another.

Reliable measures of the future supply of commercially exploitable deposits are likewise difficult to obtain. As pointed out above, technological change and new discoveries are likely to add to reserves over time. Moreover, the reserve figures reported by firms tend to have a downward bias; they are considered to be on-the-shelf inventory. Since it costs money to prove out reserves, and since taxes are in some cases based on known reserves, firms have an incentive to identify reserves only up to a certain multiple of annual production. Once assured of reserves equivalent to twenty or thirty years of production, they may stop identifying new reserves even though highly favorable prospects are readily available. (To

13. If consumption falls, secondary output could decline, but it would still increase relative to primary production and so account for a growing share of total consumption. Incentives for the recycling of many metals appear to be growing, but it should be noted that little or no prospect exists for the secondary recovery of many nonmetallic commodities, such as potash and phosphate.

offset this bias, some studies include inferred reserves along with proved reserves, but there is the possibility that some inferred deposits will be found uneconomical upon further exploration.)

If the primary production of a particular mineral product over the remainder of this century is expected to exceed its reserves, its price can be expected to rise unless there is technological change, or new discoveries, or a reduction in the price of capital, labor, energy, and the other inputs used in its production. But it does not follow that the price increase need be substantial. If, as a result of a small increase in price, the supply of the mineral (including the supply of its reserves) expands or its demand greatly contracts, the gap between reserves and cumulative production can be closed. Those familiar with nonfuel industries generally believe that the supply and demand for most of these minerals is quite responsive to changes in price over a period of five years or more.[14]

Despite the preceding caveats, it is still instructive to take another look at the reserve life expectancies shown in table 2-1. If future production is maintained at past levels, the only mineral products whose present reserves would not last through the end of this century are asbestos, diamonds, fluorspar, mercury, silver, and zinc. If future production continues to grow at the rate it has over the postwar period, bismuth, gold, and sulfur join the list. Many of the most important nonfuel minerals, such as iron ore, bauxite, phosphate rock, and potash, have sufficient reserves to last through the end of the century even if their production grows 10 percent annually.

These findings suggest that between now and the year 2000, the price of minerals (aside from those just noted) should not increase sharply because of depletion. Moreover, as a result of new discoveries, material substitution, increased recycling, and additions to reserves caused by modest price rises, even the exceptions are not likely to experience large increases in costs.

### The Twenty-first Century and Beyond

Over the long run, technological progress is essential if the cost-increasing tendencies of depletion are to be offset. Indeed, whether mineral costs rise or fall depends on the outcome of a race between technological prog-

14. In the short run—a period of a year or two—this is typically not the case. For more on the elasticities of mineral supply and demand with respect to price over the short and long run, see chapter 5.

ress and depletion. In the past, technology has won the race, and production costs have fallen; many believe this trend will continue far into the future. Others disagree. Unfortunately, there is no way to chart the future course of technological change. In light of the importance of mineral costs to the long-run welfare of mankind, however, several aspects of the depletion problem merit further examination.

First, new technology can reduce not only the private costs of the energy, labor, and capital used to find and process minerals but also can reduce the external costs, like pollution, imposed on society by mineral production and use. The recent serious concern over social costs provides strong incentives for amelioration through research and development. (Energy costs may be reduced in the same way.) Public policies can force mineral producers and consumers to internalize certain social costs, such as pollution, and prohibit other social costs, such as the destruction of the remote cultures and scenic beauty of wilderness areas. The latter policies, of course, force mineral firms to exploit other, presumably poorer, deposits, and make it more difficult for new technology to counter the upward pressure on mineral costs. But one cannot maintain that alleviating social costs inevitably results in much higher mineral prices.

Second, the faster that primary mineral production grows, the greater the burden imposed on technological change if the cost-increasing effects of depletion are to be offset. Thus, efforts toward slowing the growth of world population, reducing the intensity of per capita mineral consumption, and stimulating the recycling of mineral scrap, increase the probability that technological change will succeed in keeping mineral costs from rising. However, one cannot argue that growth in population and per capita income must cease if the adverse effects of mineral depletion are to be avoided. Conceivably, the impact of technological change could be so strong that, despite continued increases in population and income, the impact of depletion on mineral costs would be overwhelmed. It is true, as table 2-3 points out, that primary mineral production cannot continue to grow indefinitely at 10 or even 2 percent annually. But technological change provides society not just with new techniques to extract and process minerals more cheaply but also with the means to conserve mineral resources. Communication satellites that replace thousands of miles of underwater cables are but one example. Others have been noted above.

Third, the danger that depletion will force costs up varies from one mineral to another, depending on the nature of mineral ore bodies. For

Table 2-4. *Ratio of Cutoff Grade to Crustal Concentration,*
*Selected Mineral Commodities*

| Mineral commodity | Crustal concentration (ppm)[a] | Cutoff grade[b] (ppm) | Ratio |
|---|---|---|---|
| Mercury | 0.089 | 1,000 | 11,200 |
| Tungsten | 1.1 | 4,500 | 4,000 |
| Lead | 12 | 40,000 | 3,300 |
| Chromium | 110 | 230,000 | 2,100 |
| Tin | 1.7 | 3,500 | 2,000 |
| Silver | 0.075 | 100 | 1,330 |
| Gold | 0.0035 | 3.5 | 1,000 |
| Molybdenum | 1.3 | 1,000 | 770 |
| Zinc | 94 | 35,000 | 370 |
| Uranium | 1.7 | 700 | 350 |
| Carbon | 320 | 100,000 | 310 |
| Lithium | 21 | 5,000 | 240 |
| Manganese | 1,300 | 250,000 | 190 |
| Nickel | 89 | 9,000 | 100 |
| Cobalt | 25 | 2,000 | 80 |
| Phosphorus | 1,200 | 88,000 | 70 |
| Copper | 63 | 3,500 | 56 |
| Titanium | 6,400 | 100,000 | 16 |
| Iron | 58,000 | 200,000 | 3.4 |
| Aluminum | 83,000 | 185,000 | 2.2 |

Source: Earl Cook, "Limits to Exploitation of Nonrenewable Resources," *Science* (February 20, 1976).
a. Parts per million.
b. The cutoff is the lowest concentration economically recoverable in 1975.

example, as table 2-4 illustrates, mercury, silver, and certain other mineral commodities are now extracted from deposits that are so concentrated their grade exceeds the average of the earth's crust by a factor of 1,000 or more.[15] Many of these deposits also have very sharp boundaries. As these high-grade ore bodies are exhausted and producers are forced to turn to deposits with much lower grades, which some geologists suggest may be the case for certain mineral commodities, a very heavy burden will be

15. The cutoff grades shown in table 2-4 are for deposits where mineral commodities are extracted as primary products. Silver, gold, cobalt, molybdenum, and a number of other mineral commodities are now obtained in substantial quantities as byproducts or coproducts in the production of other mineral commodities, such as copper. Since all or a large part of the joint production costs in such cases can be borne by the primary product, it is often possible to produce mineral commodities profitably as byproducts or coproducts, even though their grade is below that shown in table 2-4.

placed on technological change to keep costs from rising.[16] At the other extreme, for mineral commodities extracted from deposits with concentrations not greatly different from the average of the earth's crust, such as iron, aluminum, and magnesium (not shown in table 2-4), the cost-increasing effects of depletion are likely to be much easier for technological change to cope with.

Fourth, depletion is likely to be less of a problem for those mineral products for which there are available substitutes for many of their end uses. If depletion pushes their prices up, demand will shift to other materials, primary production will drop, and pressure on costs will lessen. This presumes, of course, that the substitute materials are not also plagued by depletion and rising costs.

The substitution of new and abundant materials for relatively scarce and expensive materials is an avenue that man has used to evade depletion and scarcity since he began using iron for copper in prehistoric times. A century ago wood was widely used as both a fuel and building material. As the number of timber stands declined, the use of coal, petroleum, iron and steel, aluminum, and other alternative materials increased, relieving the pressure on available wood supplies.[17] Another and more recent example is cryolite. The only known economic deposit of this essential ingredient for aluminum production was in Ivigtut, Greenland. By 1962 it was exhausted. Considerably before 1962, however, demand from the aluminum industry outstripped the available supply, and a synthetic cryolite was developed.

Mineral commodities are rarely desired for themselves, but rather for the properties they possess, such as strength, resistance to corrosion,

---

16. A sharp drop in grade tends to push costs up because the amount of ore treated per ton of final product must rise. In addition, there may be changes in the nature of the ore for some mineral commodities that increase processing costs as grade falls below certain levels. For example, large quantities of copper, zinc, silver, nickel, gold, tin, and other scarce elements (in terms of the parts per million found in the earth's crust) are contained in common rock where they are for the most part distributed randomly as separate atoms replacing atoms of more common elements, such as magnesium or potassium. Since such low-grade ores cannot be concentrated to the levels now possible with mineral ores of higher grade, their processing costs are higher by more than the increase in ore treated per unit output, alone, requires. For more on this, see Brian J. Skinner, "A Second Iron Age Ahead?" *American Scientist,* vol. 64, no. 3 (May–June 1976), pp. 258–69.

17. See Nathan Rosenberg, "Innovative Responses to Material Shortages," *American Economic Review,* vol. 63, no. 2 (May 1973), pp. 111–18.

abrasiveness, ductility, melting temperature, electrical conductivity, malleability, weight, resistance to wear, rigidity, and appearance. In few applications is a particular material absolutely essential. As a result, when the price of a mineral commodity rises significantly, other materials are likely to be used at least for some products. This may not happen immediately, for it takes time to retool and to change manufacturing processes. Also, until they are confident that the higher prices will last, producers hesitate to make such changes, which are often expensive and disruptive. Over a period of several years, however, substitution can considerably reduce the consumption of a mineral commodity whose price is rising.

Finally, it is sometimes assumed that technological change, which has offset the adverse effects of depletion in the past, has been largely fortuitous and cannot be counted on in the future. Yet this is clearly not the case. Research and development, like other economic activities, are stimulated by the potential to earn profits.[18] As depletion increases the costs of a mineral product, it enhances the profits to be earned from the development of any new technology that makes the mineral easier to find or process, or reduces the quantity required in its end uses, or creates a substitute material. Thus, if depletion does become severe, over the long run one would expect an increasing effort to generate the technology needed to counter its adverse effects.

18. The postwar literature on the economics of technological change contains a number of studies documenting the influence of expected profitability on innovative activity. One of the most fascinating is Jacob Schmookler, *Invention and Economic Growth* (Harvard University Press, 1966). Also see Edwin Mansfield, *Industrial Research and Technological Innovation: An Econometric Analysis* (Norton, 1968).

CHAPTER THREE

# Investment and the Rise of Host Governments

THOUGH THE RESERVES of most nonfuel minerals appear ample for at least the rest of this century, shortages still could arise. It takes investment in men and facilities to find and develop the mineral deposits before the ores they contain can be extracted and processed, and there are those who believe that this investment has been inadequate and that the deficiency poses a serious threat—more serious than depletion—to mineral supplies over the next decade or two.

Although most metalliferous raw materials are now obviously in oversupply, there are many who recognize that the fall-off in mineral exploration and the lack of sufficient capital investment in new mining projects are now sowing the seeds of serious future metals shortages.[1]

A more realistic constraint on mineral supplies than resource depletion could be insufficient investment—the factor that transforms mineral occurrences into marketable supplies.[2]

The nature of mineral investment is described below. The chapter then goes on to examine the conflict over economic rents and host government

1. "Another Warning on Metals Famine to Come," *Mining Journal,* vol. 285, no. 7318 (November 21, 1975), p. 385.
2. *Trade in Primary Commodities: Conflict or Cooperation?* A tripartite report by fifteen economists from Japan, the European Community, and North America (Brookings Institution, 1975), p. 17.

participation and considers the impact of this conflict on mineral investment.

## The Nature of Investment

Investment in mining and mineral processing covers a wide range of activities. At the early end of the investment cycle comes regional exploration, which attempts to identify those specific areas within a region likely to contain ore deposits. This stage of exploration relies heavily on maps and other information already available, though aerial photographs and some geologic work on the ground may be carried out. In addition, surface waters may be analyzed for trace elements of metals, local distortions in the earth's magnetic field may be identified, and other geochemical and geophysical tests may be conducted.

Once a promising area has been found, if arrangements have not been made to acquire the property, or at a minimum the right to develop a mine, this must be done. The area involved may vary, from less than a square mile for a small high-grade gold or mercury ore body to over ten square miles for a major porphyry copper or phosphate deposit. Once the legal rights are secured, more intensive and expensive exploration follows. Roads must be built to allow personnel, equipment, and drilling supplies easy access to the site. In remote areas with rugged terrain, helicopters may fly in the equipment and temporary housing may be erected for workers. Core samples from exploratory drilling indicate whether an ore body is present and provide a preliminary estimate of its grade and size. If the results are promising up to this stage, bulk samples may be processed through a pilot plant for several months. This provides a check on the information gained from drill cores and helps determine the best metallurgical techniques to use later, in processing the ore.

During the latter stages of exploration but before the decision to develop a mine is finally made, a comprehensive feasibility study is conducted. Today this often entails sophisticated financial analyses based on present value or internal rate-of-return techniques. With the aid of computers the results are subjected to a sensitivity analysis, which shows how expected profits vary with changes in assumptions regarding future prices and costs. About the same time the feasibility study is being carried out, efforts to finance the project are undertaken. These may entail negotiations with other mining firms, banks, potential customers, international organizations such as the World Bank, and government agencies such as export-import banks. In some countries, it is also necessary to negotiate with the host government over taxes, currency convertibility, restrictions and tariffs on imports needed for the project, possible government participation in the project, and a number of other considerations.

If all of these hurdles are successfully cleared, development begins. A good access road or rail link becomes essential at this stage because of the large volume of equipment and supplies moved onto a site during development. A good communications system must also be set up; and if electric power cannot be brought in from the outside, a generating station must be constructed. If an underground mine is planned, a shaft must be sunk, hoists installed, and internal ore haulage, ventilation, power, and communications systems developed. To guide the layout of the mine, considerable development drilling must be carried out. If plans call for an open pit operation, overburden must be stripped and substantial development drilling undertaken for planning purposes. Disposal areas for tailings must also be designated and ore storage and loading facilities built.

Many ores are not rich enough to transport great distances and so are concentrated at or near the mine. This requires the construction of a mill containing crushers, ball and rod mills, flotation cells, and other equipment for upgrading the ore. Further processing may also be done at the mine site requiring the installation of smelters and refineries. At these stages, various types of facilities and technologies are used depending, among other things, on the mineral. Iron and steel, for example, are produced in blast furnaces and basic oxygen furnaces using pyrometallurgical techniques. High-purity copper and zinc are produced in electrolytic cells, and gold and silver are leached from their ores using hydrometallurgical processes.

If the mine is located in a remote region, a new town may have to be built with homes, roads, stores, medical facilities, schools, churches, a water system, and recreation facilities. A road or rail link to the sea may be needed to transport the concentrate or processed material, and new harbor facilities may be required to load the product before it is finally shipped to the customer.

Of course, many mining projects are located close enough to existing communities so that new town sites are not needed. Indeed, most new mineral investments involve just some of the activities described. Still, the description illustrates the range and diversity of activities that can be involved in finding and processing minerals. It also helps to identify and understand three very important features of mineral investment.

The first of these is the extremely large amounts of capital required at the mine development and mineral processing end of the investment cycle. The development of new mines and the construction of new smelters and refineries run into the tens of millions of dollars and with increasing frequency into the hundreds of millions of dollars. The new iron ore mine and pelletizing plant scheduled to begin production in 1977 at Fire Lake, Quebec, for example, will cost over $500 million,[3] and the Cerro Colorado copper project in Panama is now estimated at $800 million.[4] There are, of course, exceptions: tin is still recovered in Malaysia and Thailand by women panning gravel from river beds, and in Bolivia tin is produced in growing proportions by small and medium mines.[5] But for most minerals, capital costs are high and growing higher and, as a result, fixed costs constitute a large part of production costs. This is true even though energy costs, which are variable in the sense that they decline when production is curtailed, are an important component of production costs.

The second important feature of mineral investment is that new mines and processing plants are not built overnight. It takes several years after the decision is made to construct a new facility before the first ton of output is shipped, and even longer if town sites, harbors, and other support facilities have to be built. For example, estimates for the development of the Cerro Colorado copper project in Panama are over five years before production begins and over six years before planned capacity is reached (see figure 3-1). Expanding an existing copper mine, though simpler, still may take two years or more.[6] The gestation period for a new potash mine is approximately five years. Expanding an existing potash mine can take as little as one year if the mine and hoisting capacity are adequate and

3. "Quebec Venture to Get Backing of British Steel," *Wall Street Journal* (October 22, 1975), p. 10; and "1976 E/MJ Survey of Mine and Plant Expansion," *Engineering and Mining Journal,* vol. 177, no. 1 (January 1976), p. 79.

4. William E. Hoffman, "Cerro Colorado Project's Development 2 Yrs. Away," vol. 83, no. 6, *American Metal Market* (January 9, 1976), p. 2.

5. William Fox, *Tin: The Working of a Commodity Agreement* (London: Mining Journal Books, 1974), pp. 2, 58.

6. Ronald Prain, *Copper: The Anatomy of an Industry* (London: Mining Journal Books, 1975), p. 53.

Figure 3-1. *Projected Work Schedule for Development of Cerro Colorado Copper Deposit*

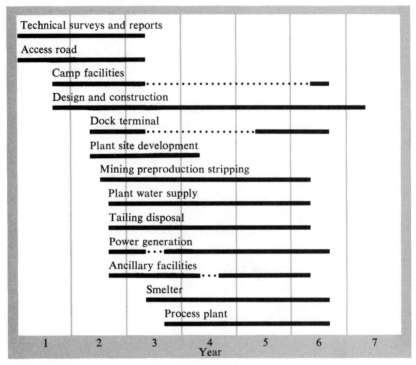

Source: David Hargrease, "Feasibility Studies Outline: Cerro Colorado Development," *Mining Magazine* (August 1974), p. 95.

only the surface plant needs to be increased, but if another mine shaft is needed the construction period is at least three years.[7]

Though adding new capacity in other mineral industries may not always take as long as that needed in the potash and copper industries, in few mineral industries can a significant project be completed in less than three years or a major expansion in less than two.[8] Feasibility studies, negotiations with the host government, and arranging financing can add to the

7. W. E. Koepke, *Structure, Behavior and Performance of the World Potash Industry,* mineral bulletin MR 139, Mineral Development Sector, Department of Energy, Mines, and Resources (Ottawa: Information Canada, 1973), p. 14.

8. Start-up dates of projects under way in the metal industries are reported in "1976 E/MJ Survey of Mine and Plant Expansion," pp. 73–86. This survey appears annually in the January issue of *Engineering and Mining Journal.*

gestation period appreciably. Construction on the Toquepala copper deposit in Peru, for example, began in 1955 following an expenditure of more than $12 million over ten years. Similarly, it took five years and over $20 million before the decision to develop the Bougainville copper deposit in Papua New Guinea was finally made in 1969.[9]

The long gestation period characteristic of mineral investments has several important consequences, one of which is that material shortages produced by inadequate investment take several years to materialize. The adverse effects of inadequate exploration are not felt until even later. Once the shortages are apparent, it is generally not possible to alleviate them quickly, since it takes several years to bring new capacity on-stream.

The third feature of mineral investment is its high risk. It is difficult to estimate the cost of developing and operating a new mine or processing facility. Development costs can change greatly during construction because of strikes and other unexpected difficulties. Problems may be encountered during the break-in period. In addition, the costs of labor, energy, and other factors of production can change between the time a project is begun and the time it is completed. A recent study of the Toquepala and Bougainville copper mines concludes that neither would have been constructed had not their costs of development and operation been seriously underestimated.[10]

The problems of predicting prices for minerals are even more formidable. For both the Toquepala and Bougainville mines estimates were far too low. Fortunately, the miscalculation of revenues more than offset the underestimation of costs, so both projects turned out to be more profitable than expected.[11]

Because of the instability of mineral markets (which chapter five examines in more detail), investors are understandably reluctant to commit the millions of dollars necessary to develop a major new mine without some assurance that once the project is completed some three to seven years in the future there will be a market for its output. Similarly, few companies are willing to make the huge capital outlays needed to construct steel furnaces, copper refineries, aluminum smelters, and other processing facilities

9. Raymond F. Mikesell, *Foreign Investment in Copper Mining: Case Studies of Mines in Peru and Papua New Guinea* (Johns Hopkins University Press for Resources for the Future, 1975), p. xviii.
10. Ibid., pp. xviii–xx.
11. Ibid.

unless they are confident of adequate supplies of raw material. This desire for assured markets and supplies, along with the increasing capital needed to develop lower grade but more massive deposits, helps explain the rise of large, vertically integrated firms in the major mineral industries during the first half of this century. As the industrialized countries became more dependent on mineral imports, mineral firms expanded their operations abroad and become international in scope. By the middle of the twentieth century, they were carrying out the bulk of the exploration for new deposits and providing the technology and capital to develop new discoveries. They owned and operated most of the mines, smelters, refineries, fabricating facilities, and distribution outlets needed to produce and market mineral products. In short, they were the principal agents through which the noncommunist world channeled new investments into the mineral sector.

As is well known, however, host governments, especially in developing countries, have increasingly challenged the dominance of the multinational mining corporations over the postwar period and particularly since the 1960s. Through their power to tax, to expropriate facilities, to impose price controls, and to establish environmental standards, host governments can affect the costs or revenues of mineral producers, perhaps curtailing development of sufficient new mineral capacity, and raising questions about the future adequacy of mineral supplies.

## The Rise of Host Governments

During the first half of the twentieth century, except when the world was at war, multinational mining corporations (hereafter called simply mining corporations) carried out their activities with a minimum of government interference. In addition, taxes were generally low. In the late 1920s, for example, the income tax on copper producers in Chile was only 12 percent, and Kennecott earned 20 to 40 percent a year on its investment in El Teniente, its Chilean mine.[12] Laws and specific agreements with host countries governing taxation, mineral rights, currency convertibility, and other important considerations affecting mining and mineral processing were seldom changed. Rarely did governments attempt to acquire a

12. Theodore H. Moran, *Multinational Corporations and the Politics of Dependence: Copper in Chile* (Princeton University Press, 1974), p. 22.

share of the equity or participate directly in their domestic mineral operations. By and large, firms were also free of requirements to purchase supplies and to carry out downstream processing domestically.

The favorable environment for mining corporations has deteriorated since World War II. The major reasons for this are not difficult to identify. The old colonial empires of Britain, France, Belgium, Holland, and Portugal have dissolved. Former colonies are now independent nation states possessing the power and authority to intervene directly in their domestic affairs. In addition, the growing sense of nationalism, found not just in the newly independent countries but throughout the world, has increased opposition to foreign control of domestic mineral production.

It is now common practice for host governments to change the conditions or ground rules under which mining corporations operate. This often occurs, for example, soon after a project has been successfully brought into production.[13] When a corporation is considering developing a mine, it is in a strong bargaining position. It has committed little or no resources to the project and could easily divert its capital and expertise elsewhere. The future profitability of the project is uncertain because of difficulties in estimating future costs and revenues. Finally, the host government seldom has the expertise needed to arrange the financing, secure the customers, supervise the construction, and overcome the problems encountered in breaking in a major new mining facility.

Once the mine is in operation, however, the uncertainty and problems surrounding a new venture are greatly reduced. At this point, if the project is a failure, the corporation writes off its losses and looks elsewhere for more promising opportunities. If the project turns out to be very profitable, however, the host government can demand a greater share of the earnings without much fear that the corporation will abandon the project, for not only are high profits being earned, but the corporation now has a substantial investment in plant and equipment, which it cannot move. If the mining corporation does opt to leave when the project is already in production and doing well, it is much easier for the host country to operate it or to find another firm to manage it.

Bougainville Copper provides a recent and interesting example of the shift in bargaining power away from the mining corporation and toward

13. For more on the obsolescing bargain, as it is called by some, see C. Fred Bergsten and others, *American Multinationals and American Interests* (Brookings Institution, forthcoming), chap. 5.

the host government, a situation that undermines the durability of negotiated agreements.[14] In 1967, before committing 400 million Australian dollars to develop the large porphyry copper deposit on the island of Bougainville, Conzinc Riotinto of Australia and New Broken Hill Consolidated negotiated an agreement governing taxes and other conditions with the government of Papua New Guinea, then a protectorate of Australia. Bougainville Copper was to enjoy an income tax holiday for the first three years of its operations and then would be allowed to write off its capital expenditures. So, depending on profitability, it would pay no income tax for five years or longer. The first year after its capital investment was completely deducted, the company was to pay the country's standard income tax rate of 25 percent. This rate would rise over four years to 50 percent, and eventually to 66 percent. At the time these terms were agreed upon, they did not appear overly favorable to the company. Indeed, internal rate-of-return calculations showed the project to be viable but far from a bonanza.

Five years later, when Bougainville Copper began operations, conditions had greatly changed. Papua New Guinea had gained its independence from Australia, and the price of copper and gold, an important byproduct of the mine, had risen sharply. As a result, the company earned a stunning 158 million Australian dollars in profits during 1973, a return equivalent to almost 40 percent of the capital invested in the project. The government did receive some of these profits, since it possessed a 20 percent equity share in the project, collected a 1.25 percent royalty on gross revenues, and imposed a withholding tax on dividends remitted abroad. However, its profits totaled only 34.6 million Australian dollars, or 22 percent of the total, a share it considered inadequate. It demanded that the 1967 agreement be renegotiated, and in 1974 Bougainville Copper agreed. The new agreement eliminated the tax holiday retroactive to the beginning of 1974, abolished the provisions allowing the company to write off all its capital investment as soon as profits permitted, and imposed an excess profits tax of 70 percent on all income over 87.2 million Australian dollars a year. These changes increase the government's share of the profits and shorten the time until it receives them. For the company the new settlement obviously reduces the return it will earn for the risk it took in searching for and developing this mine.

14. This illustration draws on Mikesell, *Foreign Investment in Copper Mining,* chaps. 6–10; and "PNG Dilemma," *Mining Journal* (October 18, 1974), pp. 330–33.

Papua New Guinea is only one of many mineral producing countries that have raised taxes on mineral producers. The Chilean government, which as noted above imposed only a 12 percent income tax on copper producers in the 1920s, increased the effective rate of taxation after World War II to such an extent that it exceeded 80 and even 90 percent of net income in some years.[15] Venezuela, Peru, Canada, Jamaica, Australia, and others have also raised taxes on their mineral producers.

Not all of the disputes between mineral corporations and host governments center on the question of taxes and the sharing of profits. Often host governments want to participate more directly in the operation of their mineral sector. They want some say in the selection of markets, the level of production, the setting of prices, the extent of domestic processing, the proportion of equity held by nationals, the employment and training of nationals, development drilling, and subsequent expansion and investment programs.

In the early 1950s, Chile was disturbed that Anaconda and Kennecott continued to sell Chilean copper in the United States at times when the U.S. producers' price was significantly below the London Metal Exchange price. To ensure that the country obtained the highest price possible for its copper, the Chilean government established a state monopoly over all copper sales, though for several reasons this experiment was short-lived. Later in the 1950s, the Mexican government encouraged the mexicanization of most mineral corporations operating in that country, by providing substantial tax benefits to those firms controlled by nationals. More recently, in the early 1970s the government of Saskatchewan imposed production and price controls on its potash producers to bolster the price. Jamaica over the last several years has refused to license new bauxite operations unless alumina facilities are also constructed. It has also tried, without complete success, to impose minimum production requirements on its producers. The Australian government intervenes directly in negotiations between its iron ore producers and the Japanese to ensure that an adequate price is paid for the country's resources.

In other cases, host governments have through nationalization simply supplanted mining corporations. Copper probably provides the best illustration. In the early 1960s, though a number of host governments were

15. The effective rate of taxation reflects the income tax plus other factors, such as foreign exchange controls. See Moran, *Multinational Corporations and the Politics of Dependence,* p. 267.

actively involved in the operations of their mineral sectors in ways described above, almost none of the noncommunist world copper came from
government-owned mines. Since then, Zaire and Chile have nationalized
all of their major mines, Zambia has acquired a controlling interest in its
major facilities, and Peru has taken over most of its mines with the important exception of Southern Peru Copper. As a result of these and other
changes, copper mines that are totally state owned account today for about
25 percent of the noncommunist world's copper, and mines in which governments have a controlling interest account for an additional 12 percent.[16] While the copper industry is somewhat unusual in terms of the
speed and extent to which nationalization has occurred, nationalization is
far from unknown in other mineral industries, as the recent expropriation
of bauxite facilities in Guyana and iron ore mines in Algeria, Mauretania,
Chile, Venezuela, and Peru illustrate.

### Conflict over Economic Rents

One of the major reasons for the increasing intervention by host governments is their desire to obtain a larger share of the profits, or economic
rents, arising from their mineral industries. The economic rent realized by
a firm from a mineral venture is the revenue it earns from the project
above the amount just required to bring it into operation or, in the case
of a project already in operation, to keep it in production. For an existing
facility, then, the economic rent the firm earns per unit of output is the
difference between the average price it receives and its out-of-pocket (or
average variable) costs of production. As long as the former exceeds the
latter, the firm will have an incentive to keep the facility in operation
even though it is not recovering capital costs.

The economic rent earned by a firm—only a part of the total generated
by a mineral venture—varies from one mineral project to another. Figure
3-2a illustrates this situation for a hypothetical mineral industry. Project
A is the mineral venture earning the greatest economic rent per unit of
output for its firm. This rent is indicated by the line $cp$. The variable costs
of this project are indicated by line $Qc$, and its output by line $QQ_1$. The
total economic rent it earns for its firm is equal to its rent per unit of output
multiplied by its output, which is reflected in the figure by the rectangle

16. Prain, *Copper: The Anatomy of an Industry*, pp. 223–24.

**Figure 3-2.** *Sources and Composition of Economic Rents for a Mineral Industry*

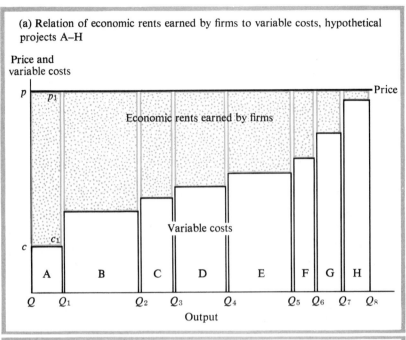

(a) Relation of economic rents earned by firms to variable costs, hypothetical projects A–H

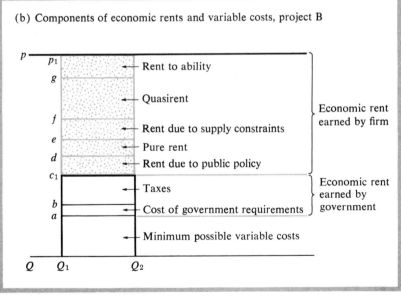

(b) Components of economic rents and variable costs, project B

$cc_1p_1p$. Project B earns the second largest rent per unit of output, project C the third, and so on; although they each realize a smaller rent per unit of output than project A, the total rent each of these projects earns for its firm may be larger than that of project A's if their output is greater.

Figure 3-2b shows the component parts of the total revenue earned by project B. The variable costs of this hypothetical project have three components: taxes, costs imposed by government requirements, and the minimum possible out-of-pocket production costs. The costs imposed by government requirements cover the increase in production expenses that arises when the firm is required to convert foreign exchange at official rather than free-market rates, to carry out downstream processing domestically even though it can be done more cheaply abroad, to purchase supplies from high-cost domestic sources, and in other ways to incur higher costs than would otherwise be necessary.[17] Thus, the host government can collect its portion of the economic rent arising from a mineral operation in two ways: first, by taxing the firm, and second, by requiring the firm to provide certain benefits to the country. In figure 3-2b, the total rents the government realizes (taxes plus benefits) per unit of output is shown as line $ac_1$.[18]

The economic rent earned by the firm (see figure 3-2b) arises from several sources. First, a firm's experience and superior knowhow can lower production costs, allowing it to realize a rent to ability.[19] Second,

17. Just why a host country should want to collect part of its rent in this way is an interesting question. For example, instead of requiring mining companies to carry out downstream processing domestically, one might argue that the country should collect its full rent in taxes and then subsidize other industries that are (1) labor intensive if unemployment is a problem, (2) skill intensive if the development of a large skilled labor force is a high priority, (3) attuned to the country's natural comparative advantage or domestic needs if foreign exchange is an important concern, (4) research and development intensive if enhancing scientific and technological capabilities is an aim, or (5) less polluting if the quality of the environment is a concern. Why countries rarely follow these courses of action is not entirely clear. It may be that government officials are unaware of their options or consider them politically infeasible. Alternatively, they may believe that mining companies are likely to resist government pressure to expand their domestic operations less than efforts to increase taxes and royalties.

18. This assumes that the government need not incur any costs to obtain these taxes and benefits. If this is not the case—if, for example, the government must provide certain services for its tax revenues such as access roads or security for the plant—then the costs of such services should be deducted from the taxes and benefits the government receives to determine its total rent.

19. For more on this as well as quasirent and pure rent see Raymond F. Mikesell

capital investment, once made, is a sunk cost, and a firm will continue to operate until the plant and equipment need to be replaced, even though the firm is not recovering its capital or earning an adequate rate of return on that capital. New firms, however, will not enter the industry unless the price is high enough to permit the recovery of capital plus a reasonable rate of return. This tends to limit supply and maintain price so that existing firms earn a quasirent that covers their average fixed costs plus a return on their investment.

Third, supply constraints may maintain the price above the level it would otherwise attain and thereby provide firms with an additional economic rent. In figure 3-2b, for example, the actual price is the amount $Q_1p_1$, while the long-run competitive price is presumed to be below this figure by the amount $ef$. In practice, the actual price may differ from the long-run competitive price for two reasons. Producers may possess monopoly or market power that allows them to restrict supply without inducing new entry even over the long run. Alternatively, in competitive industries where entry is possible, the price may rise above the long-run competitive price when demand is strong because of the time it takes to add to capacity. The excess profits this produces will stimulate new capacity and eventually cause the price to fall, but in the interim firms realize a rent because of short-run supply constraints.

Fourth, firms may earn pure rents that arise from the nature of their ore deposits. Because of grade, size, extent of overburden, ease of processing, location, or other attributes, some deposits are less expensive to exploit than others.

Finally, rents may be generated by public policy. Some mineral projects, for example, enjoy low average variable costs because their taxes are low compared to those abroad and because their host government imposes few or no requirements on them that raise their production costs. (It should be noted, however, that some projects are subject to high taxes and unfavorable policies, thereby reducing the rents they receive from other sources.)

In figure 3-2b the total economic rent per unit of output ($ap_1$) is divided between the government ($ac_1$) and the firm ($c_1p_1$), with the firm in this illustration realizing the greater share of the rents. Before World War II,

---

and others, *Foreign Investment in the Petroleum and Mineral Industries* (Johns Hopkins University Press for Resources for the Future, 1971), p. 34.

when taxes on mineral companies were modest and host governments imposed few of the restrictions that increase operating costs, the companies presumably reaped the lion's share of the rents, a situation that has changed in many countries over the last twenty-five years. This raises an important question: which components of economic rents can host governments take without adversely affecting the development of their mineral sector?

Concerning the rent stemming from public policy and the pure rent arising from high-quality deposits, one finds in many countries a strong popular sentiment that mineral wealth belongs to the people and that they, through their government, should reap all of the pure rents. This implies that the government through taxation or other means should ensure that the rent deriving from public policy is negative by an amount that just offsets the pure rent that a firm would otherwise earn.

This raises the interesting, though difficult, question of to whom the pure rents rightly belong. Should the rents associated with the rich iron ore deposits in northern Minnesota have gone to Hibbing, Eveleth, and other communities on the Mesabi Range, to the state of Minnesota, to the United States, or to an international organization? Similarly, should any rents that might be realized from the deep-sea mining of manganese nodules go to those who developed the requisite technology, to producers, to countries whose domestic mining will be most disrupted, to developing countries, or to some other group? For understandable reasons, individuals come to different conclusions in answering such questions. This has produced or aggravated many political disputes, including the recent conflict over mineral taxation between the provinces and federal government in Canada, the violent and unsuccessful attempt of Katanga to secede from Zaire shortly after Zaire became independent, and the demands of Bougainville Island for greater autonomy and even independence from Papua New Guinea.

While it is difficult or impossible to determine who is entitled to the pure rents associated with mineral deposits, it is clear that any host government that appropriates all of these rents must itself be prepared to conduct all exploration within its territory. For it is the prospect or lure of finding a particularly lucrative deposit that drives firms and individuals to search for new deposits. Once aware that they will no longer be able to reap these benefits, they will cease to look for them.

Turning to the rents deriving from supply constraints, governments can capture those temporary rents that arise when demand is high. If they do, however, they must be prepared to shoulder the losses or negative rents that accrue when price falls. Otherwise, firms will not earn an adequate rate of return over the long run and will either go out of business or move elsewhere. To a large extent, host governments already share in the benefits and the losses caused by cyclical changes in market conditions through fluctuations in the tax revenues they collect from the firms.

Under certain conditions host governments may also capture the rents that arise from supply constraints produced by market power. Specifically, if market power is based on control over available ore deposits, presumably host governments can appropriate this control from firms and use it to restrict entry, limit supply, and realize monopoly profits. However, they are unlikely to succeed in such endeavors if the market power of firms is based on other factors, such as their technology, downstream processing facilities located abroad, or access to markets. In this case, government acquisition of these rents will simply encourage firms to move elsewhere.

For a time, host governments can tax the quasirent earned by firms without affecting production. However, in the long run the firms will not recover the capital they have invested or earn a return on that investment and thus will not invest new capital in the country. As long as the existing facilities hold out and the firm is able to recover operating costs plus the rent to ability, it will remain in production, but eventually mines are exhausted and equipment must be replaced. So governments that appropriate the quasirent must be prepared either to accept the decline of their mineral industries or to assume the responsibility for new investment in this sector.

Once the host government has appropriated the rent arising from public policy, the pure rent, the rent resulting from supply constraints, and the quasirent, any attempt to take part of the rent to ability will induce firms to cease production immediately. Ability is embodied in personnel and organization, which can be moved to where they can earn a rent to ability.

Thus, unless a government wishes to drive private firms from the development of its mineral resources, the share of rents it can appropriate is limited. Unfortunately, in practice it is often difficult to determine when the host government is taking too large a share of the rents, for the adverse consequences on domestic mineral production become apparent only after several years.

*Other Reasons for Host Government Intervention*

In addition to the conflict over dividing economic rents, the growing intervention by host governments in mineral production is prompted in part by differences in economic objectives between them and the multinational mineral companies. Host governments are interested in maximizing the profits or rents of their own industries. Mining corporations strive to maximize the profits to the firm as a whole, which may require reducing production and profits in one country while increasing production and profits elsewhere. In addition, host governments, unlike mining firms, may emphasize such goals as employment and foreign exchange earnings rather than profits. There may also be differences between host governments and companies in the extent to which they prefer relatively safe and short-term projects. For example, mineral companies, particularly in politically unstable countries, may want to maximize short-run profits, even though it may entail high grading a mine or in other ways adversely affecting the long-run viability of a mineral operation.

There are political as well as economic motives behind the growing role of host governments in the development of their mineral sectors. Indeed, though often overlooked or discounted, political pressure and concerns are at times irresistible.

Many of the major mineral producing and exporting countries have only in the postwar period acquired their political independence from Britain, France, and other former colonial powers. To many of the former colonies it is an affront to their independence to have an important and highly visible sector of their economy controlled by foreign interests. How can they be truly free if foreign interests control their principal source of tax revenue and foreign exchange? Nor is this attitude confined to the newly independent states; it can be found in Latin America, Canada, Australia, and elsewhere. This concern has inspired many of the postwar demands for the training and employment of nationals, for the sharing of equity with host governments, and even for nationalization of industry. Although the economic costs may be high in terms of lost profits and rents, many countries appear willing to pay the price.

In addition, political pressure for government intervention is generated by myths or misconceptions about mineral industries, in particular, the belief that these companies make very large profits primarily from pure rents reaped by exploiting a country's geological legacy. It is true that in some years the profits earned by mineral producers are high. Earlier, it was noted that Bougainville Copper earned profits in 1973 equivalent to almost 40 percent of invested capital. This seems exorbitant until one remembers that the rate of return Bougainville Copper would have realized on its invested capital over the life of its mine would have been far smaller than 40 percent, even if the government of Papua New Guinea had not demanded a renegotiation of the tax agreement. There are two reasons for this. First, mineral markets are highly cyclical (a problem examined in chapter five), and during 1973 the demand for copper was strong and its price very high. In 1975 demand was depressed, and prices and output fell. During low-demand periods producers such as Bougainville Copper realize far smaller profits and often incur losses. Second, as pointed out earlier, Bougainville Copper invested 400 million Australian dollars over five years to develop its mine and to construct auxiliary facilities. During this period, no ore was shipped and the company earned no return on its capital. For such projects, in which large capital outlays are made over a number of years before any returns are realized, the annual profit rate must be relatively high after the project is in operation if the internal rate of return over the life of the project is to be high enough to warrant the investment.[20]

In the case of the Toquepala mine in Peru, which began operations in 1960, profits were large enough to return all invested capital by 1967–68. Still, the internal rate of return on equity, it has been estimated, was only 13.6 percent through 1972. Projecting cash flow through 1979 increases this rate to only 15 percent.[21]

Because the news media report mineral firms' high annual profit rates but rarely their more modest internal rates of return, the myth of exploitive profits is fostered, generating political pressure for intervention.

*Consequences for Investment*

Will the conflict over economic rents and the growing direct intervention of host governments stifle mineral investment and cause serious ma-

20. The internal rate of return is the discount rate that equates the present value of the future stream of costs to the present value of the future stream of revenues. Along with present-value analyses, internal rate of return is now widely used in evaluating potential mineral projects.
21. See Mikesell, *Foreign Investment in Copper Mining,* p. 73.

terial shortages some five years or so in the future? In attempting to answer this question, this section begins by examining what effects this conflict has had in the past on mineral investment[22] and then considers its impact on investment today.

In many mineral industries open conflict over rents and government participation is a relatively recent phenomenon, and it is still too early to assess the consequences for investment. In the bauxite industry, for example, only over the last few years have host governments unilaterally and substantially raised taxes and demanded other concessions from the mineral companies operating within their territories.

There are, however, a few cases that can be analyzed. Conflict between host governments and companies producing copper, for example, is found as far back as the early 1950s. In the late 1950s Venezuela sharply raised taxes on its foreign iron ore producers. Also, some data are now available on the effects of the large tax increases imposed on mineral firms in some Canadian provinces during the first half of the 1970s.

In the early postwar period, the United States, Chile, Zambia (then northern Rhodesia), Zaire (then the Belgian Congo), and Canada were the major copper producing countries outside the communist bloc. Mining corporations dominated mine production in all of these countries where, with one exception, they enjoyed a favorable investment climate throughout the 1950s. The exception was Chile. Between 1951 and 1954 the effective tax rate on the Chilean operations of Anaconda and Kennecott varied from 65 to 92 percent.[23] In addition, the government appropriated from these firms the right to market their Chilean copper, establishing a state monopoly for this purpose. The consequences for the country were severe, as Moran points out:

> Chilean strategy was becoming counterproductive. Copper production was heading lower over time, and the absolute returns to Chile from the copper sector were falling. The government had huge stocks accumulating on its hands, weak prices, and a major mine about to give out.[24]

To reverse this situation, Chile enacted new mining legislation in 1955 that greatly enhanced the investment climate. But the mining corporations,

22. This examination draws heavily on John E. Tilton, "Past and Future Patterns of World Trade in Mineral and Mining Products" (paper presented at the Conference on the Politics of Strategic Raw Materials, Swaziland, June 8–10, 1976; processed).
23. Moran, *Multinational Corporations and the Politics of Dependence,* p. 93.
24. Ibid.

apparently having lost confidence in Chile, continued to add most of their new capacity elsewhere. The only major copper producing country whose output grew more slowly than Chile's during the 1950s was the United States, where the exhaustion of high-grade deposits impeded expansion. Chile's output of copper grew at an average annual rate of 3.9 percent over this period, appreciably less than the 4.6 percent for the noncommunist world as a whole, while Canada, Zaire, and Zambia enjoyed growth rates of 5.2, 5.6, and 6.8 percent, respectively.[25] In addition, Peru and Australia, both minor producers in 1950, increased their output an average of 19.8 and 22.1 percent a year, and as table 3-1 indicates, were making substantial contributions to the world's supply of copper by 1960.

Since 1960, the investment climate for copper has deteriorated in a number of countries. Disillusioned with its 1955 mining legislation favoring mining corporations, Chile in the mid-1960s demanded the chilianization of the copper facilities run by Anaconda, Kennecott, and Cerro and in 1971 nationalized them. In Peru, as well, conflict between the government and producers led to nationalization in the early 1970s, though Southern Peru Copper, the country's largest copper producer, was spared this fate, presumably because the government wanted the company to proceed with its plans to develop the Cuajone deposit.

Zaire gained its independence from Belgium in 1960. Shortly thereafter, civil war erupted, and several years later the new government nationalized the properties of Union Miniere du Haut Katanga, the country's principal mineral producer. Zambia became independent from Britain in 1964. The new government subsequently demanded controlling interest and a greater role in the operations of its two major copper firms, Anglo American and Roan Selection Trust. More recently, the war in Angola and the embargo against Rhodesia, both countries through which Zambia ships its copper to world markets, have created serious problems for its producers.

On the other hand, conditions in the United States, Canada, Australia, the Philippines, and South Africa (including Namibia) remained relatively favorable over the 1960–75 period. These countries showed little interest in expropriation, enjoyed established and stable political systems, maintained friendly relations with neighboring states, and encouraged private investment in their mineral industries through generous tax policies. (There were exceptions: the Huk rebellion in the Philippines after

25. Growth rates cited in this paragraph are based on data in Metallgesellschaft Aktiengesellschaft, *Metal Statistics* (Frankfurt am Main, annual).

Table 3-1. *Copper Mine Production in Noncommunist World, Grade of Reserves, and Quantity of Reserves, 1960 and 1975*

| Country | Production in thousand metric tons | | Annual growth rate of production, 1960–75 (percent) | Grade of reserves, 1960 (percent) | Reserves in million metric tons | |
|---|---|---|---|---|---|---|
| | 1960 | 1975[a] | | | 1960 | 1975 |
| Philippines | 44 | 218 | 11.26 | 0.80 | 1 | 15 |
| South Africa and Namibia | 70 | 205[b] | 7.43 | 2.87 | 1 | 5 |
| Australia | 111 | 227 | 4.89 | 1.97 | 1 | 9 |
| Canada | 399 | 771 | 4.49 | 1.08 | 8 | 36 |
| Chile | 532 | 817 | 2.90 | 1.73 | 46 | 78 |
| Zaire | 302 | 426 | 2.32 | 4.44 | 25 | 18 |
| United States | 980 | 1,288 | 1.84 | 0.73 | 33 | 82 |
| Peru | 184 | 218 | 1.14 | 1.14 | 13 | 27 |
| Zambia | 576 | 662 | 0.93 | 3.59 | 20 | 27 |
| Others | 419 | 938 | 5.52 | ... | ... | ... |
| Total | 3,617 | 5,770 | 3.16 | ... | ... | ... |

Sources: 1960 production figures, Metallgesellschaft Aktiengesellschaft, *Metal Statistics, 1960–1969* (Frankfurt am Main, 1970), p. 19; 1975 production and reserve figures, U.S. Bureau of Mines, *Commodity Data Summaries 1976* (GPO, 1976), p. 47; 1960 quantity and grade of reserves, John W. Whitney, "An Analysis of Copper Production, Processing and Trade Patterns, 1950–1976" (Ph.D. dissertation, Pennsylvania State University, 1976), tables 2, 3, 4, and the sources cited there. Annual growth was calculated according to the formula 100 [(1975 production/1960 production)$^{1/15}$ − 1].

a. Production figures for 1975 are U.S. Bureau of Mines estimates.

b. This figure is for the year 1974.

World War II; increased mineral taxes and restrictions on mineral firms in Canada and Australia between 1972 and 1974; the threat of Saskatchewan to take over its potash producers; and the growing hostility that South Africa is facing from other African countries.)

Still, over most of the 1960–75 period the investment climate in these countries was favorable, and it was increasingly to these countries that mining corporations turned to develop new copper mine capacity as the situation in Chile, Peru, Zaire, and Zambia deteriorated. As a result, as table 3-1 shows, mine production in the Philippines, South Africa, Australia, and Canada grew faster than the world average between 1960 and 1975, while in Chile, Zaire, Peru, and Zambia it grew more slowly. Indeed, copper production in Zambia and Peru did not even keep pace with that of the United States where, as noted before, the lack of high-grade deposits hampered expansion. The rapid growth in the Philippines, South Africa, Australia, and Canada cannot be attributed to superior copper reserves, for, as table 3-1 indicates, the size of their reserves in 1960 were modest and the grade not particularly high. It is true that by 1975 their reserves had increased considerably, but this in large part was from the stimulating effect on exploration of their favorable investment climates.

These trends suggest that the conflict between host governments and mining corporations has significantly redirected the geographic location of new copper capacity. There is little evidence, however, that the conflict has reduced the total level of investment in new capacity. It is true that copper mine production outside the communist countries grew at an annual rate of 4.8 percent between 1950 and 1960, and then only at 3.2 percent between 1960 and 1975.[26] But this could be ascribed to a slowing of the growth in the demand for copper caused by the increased use of aluminum, plastics, and other alternative materials in the production of wire, pipe, and other important copper end uses. Moreover, if the growing conflict between host governments and mining corporations significantly stifled investment, one would expect to find either prolonged physical shortages or sharp increases in real copper prices during the 1960–75 period, neither of which occurred.

Experience in the Venezuelan iron ore industry provides further support for the hypothesis that, in the past at least, the conflict over economic

26. Ibid.

rents and host government participation changed the location of investment rather than curtailed its overall level. In the early postwar period, there was considerable concern that the world faced a growing shortage of iron ore as a result of the pending exhaustion of the high-grade Mesabi deposits.[27] Steel companies responded by searching abroad for new deposits, and in the early 1950s U.S. Steel and Bethlehem Steel began mining iron ore in Venezuela. The subsidiaries of these two firms—Orinoco Mining Company and Iron Mines Company of Venezuela—have since then accounted for nearly all of the iron ore mined in Venezuela. During the early and mid-1950s, government policy toward the foreign iron ore producers was relatively benign. In 1958, Marcos Perez Jimenez, who had controlled the country as a dictator for nine years, was deposed. Shortly thereafter, Accion Democratica, a moderate leftist party, came into power. At about this time, the government claimed that the two American subsidiaries had undercharged their parent firms for Venezuelan iron ore and thereby underpaid their taxes over the years 1953–58. The Iron Mines Company of Venezuela reached an agreement with the government in 1961 whereby it paid $19.8 million in  back taxes.[28] However, Orinoco Mining, by far the larger of the two firms, refused to pay the government claims for seven years, and in the process incurred the wrath of that country's national press and population. As the conflict escalated and became an increasingly sensitive political issue, new investment in the country's iron ore industry fell off and its share of world production declined, as shown in table 3-2. Relations between the mining companies and the government never recovered, and in 1974 the two firms were nationalized.[29]

While the Venezuelan iron ore industry stagnated in the 1960s, in Canada, Australia, Brazil, and elsewhere the pace of new investment was brisk. As a result, iron ore production during the 1960s grew worldwide as rapidly as it had in the 1950s. The conflict in Venezuela merely diverted new investment from that country to other areas.

27. For more on this see Gerald Manners, *The Changing World Market for Iron Ore, 1950–1980* (Johns Hopkins University Press for Resources for the Future, 1971), chap. 11.

28. Henry Gomez, "Venezuela's Iron Ore Industry," in Mikesell and others, *Foreign Investment in the Petroleum and Mineral Industries,* pp. 315–30.

29. For a more recent history on the evolution of the relations between the iron ore mining corporations and the Venezuelan government see Augusto J. Corrales, "Changes in the U.S. Iron Ore Market Shares held by Canada, Venezuela, and U.S. Great Lakes Region" (M.S. thesis, Pennsylvania State University, 1975).

Table 3-2. *Venezuela's Share of World Iron Ore Exports, 1951-72*

| Year | Exports in millions of metric tons | | Venezuelan exports as percent of world total |
|---|---|---|---|
| | World | Venezuela | |
| 1951 | 54.7 | 0.7 | 1.3 |
| 1952 | 61.2 | 1.7 | 3.1 |
| 1953 | 63.8 | 2.0 | 3.1 |
| 1954 | 65.5 | 5.5 | 8.4 |
| 1955 | 98.8 | 7.8 | 7.9 |
| 1956 | 116.1 | 10.9 | 9.4 |
| 1957 | 127.7 | 15.6 | 12.2 |
| 1958 | 113.6 | 15.6 | 13.7 |
| 1959 | 132.6 | 17.0 | 12.8 |
| 1960 | 153.9 | 19.3 | 12.5 |
| 1961 | 151.2 | 14.6 | 9.7 |
| 1962 | 159.1 | 13.3 | 8.4 |
| 1963 | 163.8 | 12.4 | 7.6 |
| 1964 | 196.4 | 14.9 | 7.6 |
| 1965 | 207.5 | 17.0 | 8.4 |
| 1966 | 200.0[a] | 17.0 | 8.5 |
| 1967 | 229.0[a] | 16.5 | 7.2 |
| 1968 | 253.9 | 15.0 | 5.9 |
| 1969 | 283.9 | 19.0 | 6.7 |
| 1970 | 321.2 | 21.1 | 6.6 |
| 1971 | 317.2 | 19.1 | 6.0 |
| 1972 | 312.9 | 16.5 | 5.3 |

Sources: For 1951–67, Henry Gomez, "Venezuela's Iron Ore Industry," in Mikesell and others, *Foreign Investment in the Petroleum and Mineral Industries*, p. 320; for world exports for 1968–72, U.S. Bureau of Mines, *Minerals Yearbook* (GPO, annual); for Venezuelan exports for 1968–72, Ministerio de Minas y Hidrocarburos, *1974 Petroleo y Otros Datos Estadisticos* (Caracas, 1975), p. 10.
a. Estimated.

Between 1972 and 1975 both Australia and Canada—long considered sanctuaries for mining firms—raised taxes steeply and imposed other onerous restrictions on their mineral industries. In Canada the situation has been exacerbated by the struggle between the federal and provincial governments over which was entitled to the major share of public revenues arising from the mineral sector. As a consequence, the rate of taxation jumped sharply in some Canadian provinces, particularly British Columbia and Ontario.

Since it takes several years before projects already under way are completed, it may be too early to assess the effects of rising taxes on mine development and the construction of new processing facilities. However, the impact on exploration activity is more readily apparent. Figure 3-3

Figure 3-3.  *Exploration Expenditures in Canada and Selected Provinces,*
*1968–75*[a]

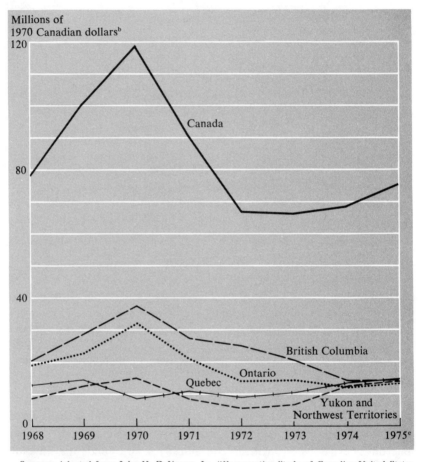

Sources: Adapted from John H. DeYoung, Jr., "Comparative Study of Canadian-United States
Resource Programs," chapter C, prepared by the Office of Resource Analysis, U.S. Geological Survey, for the Senate Appropriations Committee (USGS, March 15, 1976), table A-4; 1974 figures
and 1975 estimates are from unpublished data provided by the Canadian Department of Energy,
Mines, and Resources.
    a. Data include only general or outside exploration and exclude on-property exploration.
    b. The Canadian wholesale price index was used to calculate exploration expenditures in 1970
dollars.
    c. The figures for 1975 are preliminary.

shows exploration expenditures over the 1968–75 period for Canada as
a whole and for selected provinces in constant 1970 Canadian dollars.
From 1968 through 1970 exploration generally increased. In 1971 it de-

clined, presumably as a result of the downturn in demand and falling profits experienced by the mineral firms. Sales rebounded in 1972, 1973, and early 1974, however, and exploration activity began to recover in Canada as a whole, in Quebec (where the provincial tax increase came after 1974), and in the Yukon and Northwest Territories (which are administered by the federal government, so that intergovernmental confrontations over mineral rents are not a problem). But in those provinces where the tax hikes were the greatest—British Columbia and Ontario— exploration actually continued to decline over the 1972–74 period before beginning a small upturn in 1975.

On the basis of claims staked and other information, it appears that while mineral exploration was down in British Columbia it increased in the nearby American states of Washington, Idaho, and Montana, as well as Alaska.[30] Canadian mining companies conducted an estimated 60 percent of their exploration effort outside of Canada in 1975 compared with 20 percent in 1971.[31] Apparently, exploration activity by Canada's mining enterprises has been not stifled but redirected, both within Canada and without.

While the available information suggests that the conflict over rents and host government participation has not yet seriously affected the overall level of investment in the mineral sector, there is concern about the future. As more countries demand higher rents and taxes one might ask whether mineral corporations will continue to find countries with favorable investment conditions. The investment climate in Canada and Australia has changed. In South Africa, the long run is clouded by the possibility of conflict with neighboring states over the issue of white minority rule. And in the United States and other industrialized countries, as the next chapter points out, environmental regulations, withdrawal of public lands from exploration and mineral development, inflation, price controls, and other factors are creating uncertainty and could discourage investment in the mineral sector.

If the investment environment is deteriorating everywhere, what will prevent this situation from simply choking off the development of new

30. John H. DeYoung, Jr., "Comparative Study of Canadian-United States Resource Programs," chapter C, prepared for the Office of Resource Analysis, U.S. Geological Survey, for the Senate Appropriations Committee (USGS, March 15, 1976), pp. 61–63.

31. Ibid., p. 33.

mineral projects? While the possibility of some adverse effect on investment cannot be ruled out, the serious consequences envisaged by some
are probably exaggerated for several reasons.

First, over the last decade mineral corporations have adopted techniques that (a) reduce the probability that the host government will unilaterally expropriate a mineral venture or impose confiscatory taxes and
(b) alleviate the consequences for the firms involved if it does. Traditionally, mineral corporations have financed the development of mineral projects largely out of their own capital. In addition, the parent company has
guaranteed the obligations of its subsidiaries, so that lenders do not have
to concern themselves with the viability of individual projects except to
the extent that they could threaten the overall solvency of the parent company.

In the latter 1960s, more and more mineral corporations turned to
project financing, following the successful use of this technique by Kennecott in Chile.[32] With project financing, the project stands or falls on its
own. Parent companies are typically liable only for the capital they have
committed to the project. There is also much heavier reliance on debt
financing. For example, the Freeport Mineral Company and the other
owners of the Ertsberg mine, which began producing copper in Indonesia
in the early 1970s, provided only $24 million of the $146 million invested
in the venture.[33]

In addition, an attempt is often made to diversify the number and location of debt and equity holders. This characteristic of project financing is
well illustrated by the Mineracoes Brasileiras Reunidas iron ore project in
Brazil. Equity is shared by the Brazilian holding company Cia Auxiliar de
Empresa de Mineracao (31 percent);[34] Hanna Mining Company, a U.S.
firm (25 percent); a consortium of six Japanese steel companies and
five Japanese trading companies (10 percent); Universe Tankships, a

32. For an interesting account see Theodore H. Moran, "Transnational Strategies
of Protection and Defense by Multinational Corporations: Spreading the Risk and
Raising the Cost for Nationalization in Natural Resources," *International Organization,* vol. 27, no. 2 (Spring 1973), pp. 273–87.

33. James Michael Biello, "New Financing Strategies for International Mining
Projects" (M.S. thesis, Pennsylvania State University, 1975), p. 38.

34. Although it contributed only 31 percent to the equity, a multilayered financial arrangement allows this firm to control the project. Thus, the project is controlled by Brazilian interests. This and other data in the paragraph are from ibid.,
pp. 21–22.

Liberian firm that will transport a portion of the ore (10 percent); and a number of minority shareholders (24 percent). Together, these sources provided $30 million. In addition, $158 million in debt was raised from a consortium of Japanese banks (13 percent), a consortium of American banks (16 percent), the World Bank (31 percent), the Japanese Export-Import Bank (23 percent), and the U.S. Export-Import Bank (17 percent).

Other common features of project financing include long-term contracts to ensure a market for the project's output and thus an adequate cash flow to service its debt; insurance against expropriation, purchased from such government agencies as the U.S. Overseas Private Investment Corporation (OPIC); and host government guarantees for loans from the World Bank and other sources.

While project financing raises the cost of capital for mineral projects, it appreciably reduces the risk borne by any one firm by spreading it over a large number of equity and debt holders. In addition, it greatly increases the cost to the host country of unilaterally abrogating its commitments, for such an action would provoke reactions world wide from banks, from consuming firms with long-run contracts, from producing firms involved with the project, from government agencies such as export-import banks and OPIC, and from international organizations such as the World Bank. Moreover, if the host government has guaranteed the project's obligations, failure to honor these commitments may lead to the confiscation of that country's property in other countries. After Chile expropriated Kennecott's El Teniente mine, Kennecott used such a guarantee to obtain a writ of attachment against Chilean property in the United States, including Lanchile jets that landed in the country.[35] Only after the Chilean government promised to pay its obligations did the firm relent.

Second, the growing participation of host governments in new mineral projects should reduce the adverse effects on investment of the conflict over economic rents and host government intervention. It is now increasingly common for governments to acquire a share of the equity of new projects. The government of Papua New Guinea, for example, owns 20 percent of Bougainville Copper; the government of Guinea owns 49 percent of the Boké bauxite project; the government of Dominican Republic owns 9.5 percent of the Falconbridge Dominicana nickel project; and the

35. Moran, "Transnational Strategies of Protection and Defense by Multinational Corporations," p. 282.

Quebec government's steel producing agency, SIDBEC-NORMINES, owns a controlling interest in the new iron ore facility being developed at Fire Lake, Quebec. Such arrangements help defuse the hostility toward foreign firms found in many countries. Where government officials serve on the board of directors, management is more aware of the concerns of the state and is less likely to blunder with sensitive political issues. At the same time, the government becomes cognizant of the problems confronting the firm, its need for security and an adequate rate of return, as well as the options it has if these needs are denied.

Finally, the aspiration of nearly all countries well endowed with mineral resources to use those resources to further their own development is a strong force for the prevention of serious capacity shortages. Policies that stifle new mineral investment reduce the contribution that this sector can make to a country's welfare and are unlikely to be pursued for long. A recent illustration is provided by Canada and Australia, which now appear to be backing away from the high taxes and other restrictions imposed on their mineral producers over the 1972–74 period. The realization that these measures were deterring new investment and thus undermining the long-run strength of their mineral industries is responsible in large part for the change. Similarly, Chile and Zaire have shown renewed interest in attracting private investment in their mineral sectors over the last several years.

Some have even argued that the desire of many countries to use their mineral wealth to promote economic development may lead to oversupply rather than undersupply, as host governments gain increasing control over their mineral resources. In the words of Ronald Prain who ran Roan Selection Trust in Zambia over most of the postwar period:

> As more and more projects are now being initiated all over the world as part of national development programmes, there is a danger that mining development may come to be dictated more by the needs of national economy than by market considerations. Whether the mining industry is in the public or private sector, the pressure from governments to bring into production not only copper but other national resources as quickly as they can be found can be intense, and the old prudent practice of putting an ore body "on ice" until economic conditions generally favour its exploitation tends to be abandoned in the rush to market.

This trend towards the adoption of a "discover-and-develop" philosophy has, not surprisingly, been most noticeable in the developing countries.[36]

36. Prain, *Copper: The Anatomy of an Industry*, pp. 205–06.

Since new mineral ventures provide jobs, skill training, government revenues, and foreign exchange, as well as generate business for domestic suppliers and downstream processors, host governments may be willing to develop projects whose expected profit or internal rate of return falls below the level considered adequate by private enterprises. Bolivia, for example, has for a number of years subsidized uneconomic tin mines because of their importance to the country's economy and the political repercussions from allowing them to collapse. The same is true for a number of nationalized steel industries. Thus, as more and more of the production of copper and other mineral commodities comes under the direct control of host governments, the possibility of oversupply cannot be ruled out.

In the immediate future, it is true, the ability of most host governments to develop major new mineral projects is limited, for few now possess the necessary expertise and technical capability, even assuming they can arrange the financing. As noted earlier, it is far easier to take over an ongoing operation than to develop a new one. Still, over the postwar period many governments have acquired the technical skills to monitor and even run their domestic mineral industries, and it would appear to be only a matter of time before they gain the requisite talent needed to develop new projects. Moreover, in the interim, they may be able to buy the necessary services from private mining corporations and others. Panama, for example, is planning to rely on the expertise of Texasgulf to develop its massive Cerro Colorado copper project. The American firm is to receive a 15-year management contract plus 20 percent of the equity (the rest to be held by Panama), with Panama reserving the option to buy out Texasgulf's share after 20 years.[37] The large copper mine being developed at Sar-Cheshmeh is entirely owned by the Iranian government. Anaconda has a 14-year service contract to develop and operate the mine. The company is required to recruit and train Iranians so that the project can be entirely run by nationals by the end of the contract period.[38]

Such arrangements suggest that host governments will in the future be increasingly taking the initiative in the development of new mineral ventures, offsetting any tendency on the part of mineral corporations to reduce their investment activity.

37. "Texasgulf, Panama Signs 2 Pacts Tied to Cerro Colorado Project," *American Metal Market,* vol. 83, no. 40 (February 27, 1976), p. 44.

38. "Progress at Sar-Cheshmeh Copper Mine, Iran," *Mining Magazine* (March 1975), p. 183.

CHAPTER FOUR

# Investment and the Environment, Energy, and Capital Availability

THE LAST CHAPTER looked at the investment problems created by the rising power of host governments and the conflict over economic rents and host government participation. The conflict tends to be greatest in the developing countries. This chapter focuses on public policies and government actions found in the United States and other developed countries that may threaten new investment in the mineral sector and sow the seeds of future material shortages.

## The Environment and Energy

The late 1960s and early 1970s saw the rise of the environmental movement in the United States and other industrialized countries. Mining and mineral processing by their nature are polluters. They disturb land, dump tailings, emit sulfur and other pollutants into the air, and dispose of wastes into waterways. Thus environmental regulations, which have grown increasingly strict over the last decade, along with related regulations on occupational safety and health, have a major impact on mineral industries.

54

In particular, these regulations affect mineral investment. They increase the capital needed for new projects and require that a significant portion of mineral investment go for pollution abatement at existing facilities. The American steel industry, for example, estimates that between 1975 and 1983 it will spend $9 billion or about 20 percent of its total capital expenditures on pollution control equipment at existing plants.[1] Environmental and safety regulations also increase the uncertainty associated with mineral investments because they are frequently changed and because the regulations at the federal, state, and local levels are in some instances conflicting and inconsistent. Thus, firms cannot be certain that a new facility planned today will meet environmental and safety standards in effect several years hence, when it is scheduled to begin production.

These effects have led some to conclude that the environmental movement seriously threatens to curtail the expansion of mineral production capacity. In support of this position, it is sometimes argued that environmental regulations forced a 40 percent reduction in American zinc smelting capacity in the early 1970s. However, the smelters that shut down were old facilities based on obsolete technology. Environmental regulations may have been the straw that broke the camel's back, but these plants would soon have closed for other reasons.[2]

Not only is the empirical evidence weak, but more fundamentally it is not clear conceptually why greater costs and uncertainty should discourage investment as long as firms can raise prices to cover the higher costs and obtain compensation for their greater risk. It is true that higher prices are likely to dampen demand and may in this way reduce the expansion of capacity. But this presumably is desirable to the extent the decline in demand occurs because consumers bear the full costs of mineral materials, including the environmental costs. It is possible that environmental regulations may divert investment from the United States (and other countries where these restrictions are severe) to countries where concern over the environment is less and restrictions are more lenient. However, it is difficult to find good examples of such diversion; and as the following quotation by Mikesell suggests, it does not appear of great importance:

1. See Frederick M. Thayer, Jr., "The Capital Formation Challenge Facing the Steel Industry," *Fourth National Seminar: Steel Industry Economics,* 1975 Report of Proceedings (American Iron and Steel Institute, 1975), p. 19.
2. Barry A. Hillman, "Investment in the Zinc Industry, 1950–1970" (Ph.D. dissertation, Pennsylvania State University, forthcoming).

Virtually all copper industry officials with whom I have talked agree that differences in pollution abatement costs are likely to be too small in relation to the large number of uncertain factors associated with foreign investment to make an appreciable difference in their decision regarding a foreign investment in most developing countries.[3]

Related to the environmental movement is the growing withdrawal of federal lands in the United States from mineral activity, a development some see undermining future mineral investment. In the continental United States about one-fifth of the land is owned by the federal government. When Alaska is included, the figure is one-third. Historically, most of this territory has been open to mineral exploration and development by private firms and individuals. The Mining Law of 1872, which still governs the exploitation of most of the valuable nonfuel minerals on federal lands, allows private individuals and firms to work mineral deposits under quite favorable terms. No royalties or special taxes, for example, are imposed. Nor are leases sold. The finder of a deposit merely has to demonstrate that it is economic and to carry out a minimum of development work to obtain the right to exploit it.

Over the years, certain federal lands have been set aside for military reservations, national parks, and other purposes, and on these lands exploration and development are no longer permitted. Up to 1968 such withdrawals covered only 17 percent of all public lands, but since then this figure has jumped markedly. In a recent article that has received considerable attention, Bennethum and Lee report that 53 percent of public lands were formally closed to exploration and development by 1974.[4] In addition there are areas where mineral firms are still legally permitted to operate but where they have little or no incentive to do so because the restrictions on their activities are too severe. In some cases, for example, they cannot build roads or use motorized vehicles. If these lands are excluded, the figure increases from 53 to 67 percent.

These findings have produced considerable concern that piecemeal public policies governing federal lands are adversely affecting mineral exploration, and eventually may contribute to material shortages. However, a close look at the figures presented by Bennethum and Lee, as they

3. Raymond F. Mikesell, "The Impact on U.S. Trade and Foreign Investment of EPA Environmental Abatement Regulations on the Copper Industry" (August 1975; processed), p. 49.

4. Gary Bennethum and L. Courtland Lee, "Is Our Account Overdrawn?" *Mining Congress Journal,* vol. 61, no. 9 (September 1975), p. 35.

themselves point out, indicates that the vast majority of the acres withdrawn from mineral use during the 1968–74 period were in Alaska as a result of the Alaskan Native Claims Settlement Act of 1971. This act accounted for 250 million acres, or 89 percent of the 281 million acres excluded from mineral exploration and development over this period. A sizable portion of this acreage will be reopened for mineral activity after the Alaskan natives have chosen 40 million acres to which they are entitled under the act and after the state and federal governments have completed their selection of acreage for parks, wildlife refuges, and other purposes. Furthermore, the land acquired by the natives, though no longer owned by the government, may still be open to exploration and development.[5]

These considerations suggest that, although the government has withdrawn considerable acreage of federal lands over the last eight years, the impact on mineral investment has been exaggerated. A large part of this territory will eventually be reopened to mineral producers. In addition, much of the withdrawn land is in Alaska. Given its remoteness and harsh climate, a great deal of new mineral development would probably not occur in much of this region even in the absence of land withdrawals. Finally, and perhaps most important, as long as depletion is not a serious problem, as argued in chapter two, there are deposits elsewhere to which mineral producers can turn for exploration and development.

Another area of public policy causing considerable concern is energy. In 1973 the Arab oil-exporting countries imposed an embargo on petroleum shipments to the United States and the Netherlands. When the embargo ended, prices were unilaterally raised to artificially high levels by the Organization of Petroleum Exporting Countries. In response to these shocks and other problems in the energy area, the major importing countries have attempted to formulate and implement new national energy policies. In the United States, for example, public policy is now striving to promote greater energy self-sufficiency. Just what this will eventually mean for tariffs or quotas on oil imports, for the deregulation of natural gas prices, and for the domestic price of energy in general is far from clear.

Since many of the mineral industries are heavy consumers of energy, there is concern that higher and more uncertain energy prices may deter new mineral investment. However, here—as in the case of environmental regulations—production should satisfy consumer needs as long as consumers are willing to compensate producers for higher energy costs and

5. Ibid., pp. 38–40.

for increased risk in developing new mineral projects. If higher prices do depress demand and the rate at which new capacity is built, it would be an adjustment that is desirable, for it would reflect the fact that consumers faced with higher priced mineral products would rather spend more of their income on other commodities.

## The Availability of Capital

In an era when the demands on the capital market from other sectors, particularly energy and communications, are climbing rapidly, a question asked with increasing frequency is where the funds required for an adequate expansion of capacity in the nonfuel mineral sector will come from. This section examines the possibility that a shortage of capital will prevent the development of adequate new mineral capacity. It begins by examining the prospects for a general capital shortage and then the possibility that the mineral sector may suffer a capital shortage even if the economy as a whole does not.

### Prospects for a General Capital Shortage

The last several years have witnessed considerable concern over the possibility of a future capital shortage for the economy as a whole. Any general shortage of funds would certainly adversely affect investment in the mineral industries, given their great capital requirements and their growing dependence on the debt and equity markets for their capital needs.

A number of studies have been conducted on the capital requirements and availability of savings for the United States over the next five to ten years.[6] Although the studies come to different conclusions regarding the likelihood of future capital shortages, they do project similar private capital requirements, equivalent to just over 15 percent of the gross national product. They also tend to agree on the level of consumer and business savings. Where differences arise is in projections of future government savings. In short, they suggest that, if a capital shortage is to be avoided in the future, the government sector cannot continue to run substantial

6. For a comparison of several of these studies see Henry C. Wallich, "Is There a Capital Shortage?" *Challenge* (September/October 1975), pp. 30–36.

deficits. If state and local governments rely heavily in the future on borrowed funds, as many expect, the federal government must run a sizable surplus. Thus, the debate over whether or not the country faces a general capital shortage centers primarily on the likelihood that the federal government will realize a budget surplus. While in theory at least the government can easily produce a surplus, either by raising taxes or reducing federal expenditures, those who predict a capital shortage argue that it is politically naive to assume it will actually do so.

## Capital for the Mineral Sector

Even if a general capital shortage is averted, the mineral sector may still face difficulties raising the capital it needs for future expansion. The mineral industries are particularly vulnerable to changes in the business cycle, as discussed in the next chapter. During depressed conditions, output and often prices tend to fall substantially, forcing down profits. During such periods, it is not uncommon for mineral producers to incur sizable losses.

Since a temporary downturn caused by the business cycle in no way affects the long-run need for new mineral capacity, and since it takes several years for new capacity to be built and brought on-stream, the desired level of new investment in this sector presumably should not fall or rise with short-term changes in the business cycle. Yet even a casual reader of the trade press quickly becomes aware of the impact that short-run business trends have on mineral investment. The 1975 annual report of the Bethlehem Steel Corporation, for example, reported:

With 1975 earnings adversely affected by increased costs and the decline in shipments, we took action last fall to stretch out our capital spending program by extending the completion dates of various projects by one to two years.

The principal projects affected by the stretch-out are the 8,000 ton per day blast furnace at the Sparrows Point Plant, which is now scheduled to be completed in mid-1979 instead of late 1977; the 110 inch plate mill, third BOF vessel and light flat-rolled facilities at the Burns Harbor Plant, which have been extended one to two years beyond their original completion dates; the expansion of the Hibbing taconite project, which will be completed in 1979 instead of 1978; and various coal mining projects in Pennsylvania and West Virginia, which have been extended one or two years beyond their original completion dates.

During the upswing in the economy in 1973 and early 1974, many new

Table 4-1. *Number of Investment Projects in the Aluminum, Copper, and Nickel Industries, 1973–75*[a]

| Nature of project | Number of new projects announced during | | | Number of projects cancelled, postponed, or stretched out during | | |
|---|---|---|---|---|---|---|
|  | *1973* | *1974* | *1975* | *1973* | *1974* | *1975* |
| *Aluminum* | | | | | | |
| Mine[b] | 2 | 2 | 0 | 0 | 0 | 1 |
| Smelter | 19 | 9 | 10 | 2 | 6 | 14 |
| Refinery | 8 | 3 | 9 | 1 | 1 | 2 |
| Other[c] | 4 | 1 | 4 | 1 | 0 | 4 |
| Total | 33 | 15 | 23 | 4 | 7 | 21 |
| *Copper* | | | | | | |
| Mine[b] | 25 | 26 | 8 | 2 | 5 | 7 |
| Smelter | 8 | 3 | 1 | 1 | 1 | 2 |
| Refinery | 5 | 3 | 4 | 1 | 1 | 1 |
| Other[c] | 8 | 6 | 7 | 1 | 0 | 3 |
| Total | 46 | 38 | 20 | 5 | 7 | 13 |
| *Nickel* | | | | | | |
| Mine[b] | 5 | 4 | 0 | 1 | 2 | 0 |
| Smelter | 2 | 1 | 2 | 0 | 0 | 0 |
| Refinery | 2 | 3 | 1 | 0 | 1 | 1 |
| Other[c] | 1 | 6 | 1 | 2 | 1 | 3 |
| Total | 10 | 14 | 4 | 3 | 4 | 4 |

Sources: Based on information found in "Survey of Mine and Plant Expansion," *Engineering and Mining Journal* (January issues 1973–76).

a. Projects in communist countries and projects in initial proposal stage are excluded.

b. This category includes projects identified as mines, mines with plants, mines with concentrators, mines with complexes, concentrators, and concentrators with plants.

c. This category includes projects identified as complexes, concentrators and complexes, mines with refineries, mines with smelters, smelters and refineries, and plants.

projects were announced. Since then, as table 4-1 indicates for aluminum, copper, and nickel, fewer new projects have been launched and a number of those announced earlier have been canceled, postponed, or stretched out, even though the economy may be booming and much in need of their capacity at the time they were scheduled to begin production.

One reason for this behavior, which can contribute to short-run supply and demand imbalances in the future, is simply the fact that mineral firms find it much harder and more expensive to raise capital during depressed conditions. These firms generate capital from three primary sources: retained earnings, debt, and new equity issues. When profits are down or negative, internally generated funds for expansion shrink, largely because revenues are lower but also because inventory-carrying costs tend to rise as unsold stocks accumulate. Stock prices are also depressed during such periods, making managers reluctant to issue new equity for fear of diluting the control and earnings of existing stock holders. Finally, access to debt funding is more restricted when profits are down and has become increasingly so over the last twenty years for mineral firms whose debt-equity ratios have increased above those levels considered prudent. Even those firms that can borrow substantial amounts when their profits and stock are depressed often hesitate to do so for fear the credit rating institutions, such as Moody's Investor Sources and Standard and Poor, will revise their bond ratings downward.

Just why the stock and capital markets are so heavily influenced by current conditions rather than the long-run profit potential of firms is not entirely clear. Apparently, future expectations are heavily influenced by the present. Such myopia may also prompt firms to reassess the potential of projects that they in better times approved. If so, this may reinforce the tendency to cut back on investment when business is down and capital is difficult to raise.

The propensity of firms and financial institutions to allow present conditions to affect future expectations also raises the possibility that the recent rapid inflation in construction costs of new mineral projects may impede an adequate level of investment. Between the early 1950s and 1970, the capital costs for building a ton of new copper capacity increased from $1,300 to $3,000, or between four and five percent a year.[7] Since then construction costs have increased at two to three times this rate, and interest rates have risen as well. Major new copper projects, as a result, now require a copper price of at least 90 cents a pound,[8] and many financial institutions appear reluctant to invest in projects whose financial viability requires such high prices (by historical standards). Yet if the supply of copper is to grow, new deposits will have to be developed, and presumably the price of copper will have to rise.

Another aspect of macroeconomic policy that can threaten the ability of mineral firms to obtain sufficient capital for expansion is price controls. The experience of the American steel industry illustrates this possibility.

7. Ronald Prain, *Copper: The Anatomy of an Industry* (London: Mining Journal Books, 1975), p. 186.

8. See, for example, the statement attributed to Simon D. Strauss in William E. Hoffman, "Asarco Exec Calls Hope Slim for Int'l Copper Price Accord," *American Metal Market* (April 2, 1976), pp. 2, 5.

Since steel is an important and basic commodity, steel prices are thought to have a major effect on the rate of inflation, and attempts by the industry to raise prices receive considerable public and governmental scrutiny. On numerous occasions, the American government has cajoled, pressured, and coerced the industry either to not implement increases or to reduce the size of those it had announced (the confrontation between President Kennedy and U.S. Steel's president, Roger Blough, in 1962 being perhaps the most dramatic). Formal price controls, previously used only during military conflicts, have also been used, starting with the general wage and price freeze in 1971 and continuing with the controls imposed during 1973 and early 1974.

Although government has tried to influence steel prices more than other mineral prices, these others have not escaped such pressure entirely, particularly during the last few years. They were included under the price controls imposed between 1971 and 1974, and in earlier periods the government urged moderation in price rises, suggesting that releases from the strategic stockpiles held by the country might otherwise be necessary. Nor is the United States the only country in which the government intervenes directly to reduce the pace of price increases in the mineral sector, as the recent price controls in Britain and Canada illustrate.

Thus, over the postwar period, one finds numerous examples of government actions to hold down mineral prices during periods of high economic activity. At first, these efforts were largely concentrated on steel but have over time spread to other minerals as well. In addition, the use of formal controls, rather than moral suasion, appears to be growing.

Given the volatility of profits during the business cycle, which for reasons examined in the next chapter tends to be more severe for mineral producers than for most other firms, mineral firms must be able to earn high profits during the boom phase of the cycle if they are to earn an adequate rate of return over the entire cycle. While this may require that they raise prices when demand is strong and thereby aggravate inflation, if these firms cannot earn a rate of return over the cycle comparable to that of other enterprises, they will have neither the incentive nor the ability to raise the capital needed to expand capacity to meet future needs. Ironically, shortages that arise for this reason could be falsely attributed to the industry's ineptness and lead to even more government intervention.

In summary, the mineral sector appears to be coping reasonably well with many of the potentially disruptive influences on investment. According to the last chapter, the major mining and mineral processing firms have responded to the growing conflict over economic rents and host government participation by redirecting their investment to safer countries and by developing new financing techniques, which reduce the level of risk and distribute it over many more investors. Similarly, environmental and safety regulations, federal land withdrawals in the United States, and energy policies, though they have raised production costs do not appear to have restricted greatly the overall level of investment in the mineral sector.

A more serious threat to mineral investment is price controls. Used increasingly by governments to cope with inflation, price controls can undermine the profitability of mineral firms and thus their ability to raise capital. Rising construction costs and interest rates can also cause short-run problems in raising funds, as can falling demand, with its falling profits and stock prices. Thus, if investment is inadequate, the culprit is likely to be the cyclical volatility that plagues the mineral sector. Investment difficulties would likely diminish if cyclical volatility could be reduced.

# CHAPTER FIVE

# Cyclical Volatility

As EARLIER CHAPTERS have noted, the mineral industries frequently encounter short-run imbalances between supply and demand, which create sharp fluctuations in output and profits and, in some cases, prices. For a year or two, and sometimes even longer, these short-run disturbances can produce severe shortages either in the sense that the available supplies are inadequate to satisfy demand at the prevailing price or in the sense that sharp price increases are required to constrain demand to the available supply.

Some might argue that such shortages are caused by insufficient capacity and thus are really just another aspect of the adequacy of investment, examined in the last chapter. Yet given the high capital costs of most mineral production and the resulting expense of carrying idle capacity, the optimal solution to the cyclical volatility problem probably does not lie in building sufficient capacity to meet all short-run peaks in demand. Before other possible measures for coping with the cyclical volatility problem can be assessed—a task left to chapter seven—it is necessary to examine the causes and the consequences of cyclical volatility.

## The Causes of Cyclical Volatility

Cyclical volatility arises largely as a result of three characteristics of mineral supply and demand. The first is the unresponsiveness of supply in the short run to changes in price—what economists call the low short-run price elasticity of supply—once the available capacity is being fully used. As long as excess capacity exists, mineral producers can expand supply easily and quickly, and over this range of output supply responds to increases in price quite well. As output approaches full capacity, however, increasing it becomes more difficult even with prices climbing substantially. As chapter three points out, it often takes four years or longer to develop major new mines and two or three years to expand existing facilities.

The second important characteristic is the low short-run price elasticity of demand, which reflects the fact that changes in price do not greatly affect demand, either, in the short run. There are two reasons for this. First, mineral products generally are intermediate goods whose demand is ultimately derived from final or consumer products. In most cases, the cost of the mineral products used in the production of final goods constitutes only a small fraction of the latters' cost. For example, prices of the cold rolled steel sheet used in refrigerators, of the copper used in outboard motors, and of the aluminum used in modern office buildings can jump sharply and yet cause only a small increase in the final cost of the end product. As a result, even if the price elasticity of demand for the end product is high, that for the intermediate mineral product tends to be low. Second, while the producers of most final goods can substitute one material for another and thereby increase the elasticity of demand for mineral commodities, rarely can it be done on short notice. The use of alternative materials often requires ordering new equipment, changing the existing layout of a fabricating facility, and retraining workers. Moreover, given the costs involved, producers hesitate to undertake such substitutions until they are confident that the price change will last.

For a number of years attempts have been made to calculate the price elasticities of supply and demand for various minerals.[1] Table 5-1 shows

1. More recently, price elasticities have been estimated using econometric techniques. However, many of these efforts are still plagued by specification and other problems, and consequently the validity of their estimates are open to question. For example, one of the more imaginative and interesting models found that the long-run elasticity of supply for copper was 0.40 in Chile, 1.67 in the United States, 14.84 in Canada, and either negative or infinite for Zambia, depending on how one interprets an obviously perverse result. See Franklin M. Fisher, Paul H. Cootner, with Martin N. Baily, "An Econometric Model of the World Copper Industry," *The Bell Journal of Economics and Management Science,* vol. 3, no. 2 (Autumn 1972), pp. 576–79.

Table 5-1. *Price Elasticities of Demand, Selected Mineral Commodities*[a]

| Mineral commodity | Short run (1 year) | Intermediate run (3–5 years) | Principal substitutes |
|---|---|---|---|
| Aluminum-bauxite | −0.13 | −0.80 | Copper, steel, wood, plastics, titanium |
| Chromite | 0 to −0.2 | Elastic | Nickel, molybdenum, vanadium |
| Cobalt | −0.68 | −1.71 | Nickel |
| Copper | −0.3 | Elastic | Aluminum, plastics |
| Lead | Inelastic | Elastic | Rubber, copper, plastics, tile, titanium, zinc |
| Mercury | Inelastic | −1.0 | ... |
| Molybdenum | Inelastic | n.a. | Tungsten, vanadium |
| Platinum-palladium | 0 to −0.1 | −0.4 to 0.9 | Gold |
| Tungsten | −0.15 | −0.3 | Molybdenum |
| Zinc | −0.55 | −0.67 | Aluminum, plastics |

Source: Testimony of James C. Burrows, vice president, Charles River Associates, Inc., in *Outlook for Prices and Supplies of Industrial Raw Materials*, Hearings before the Subcommittee on Economic Growth of the Joint Economic Committee, 93:2 (GPO, 1974), p. 71.

n.a. Not available.

a. Price elasticity of demand is the percentage decrease in demand produced by a 1 percent increase in price. If a 1 percent increase in price causes less than a 1 percent decrease in demand, demand is considered inelastic (price elasticity of demand between 0 and −1).

demand elasticities estimated by Charles River Associates, a research firm with considerable experience in the minerals field. As expected, in the short run (defined as a year) the elasticities are very low. Over the intermediate run (three to five years), they are appreciably higher, and presumably over the long run (more than five years) would be even higher.

The responsiveness of supply to small increases in price, until existing capacity is fully utilized, and the unresponsiveness of supply in the short run to increases in price, thereafter, indicate that the supply curves for minerals tend to rise gradually until full capacity is reached and then become very steep. The unresponsiveness of demand for mineral products in the short run implies that the demand curve will be steep throughout its entire range. While the peculiar slopes of the short-run supply and demand curves do not by themselves create cyclical volatility, they do set the stage, for now a shift in either of these curves will produce large changes in output, price, or both (as shown in figure 5-2). This, in turn, is likely to produce large fluctuations in profits.

The third important characteristic of mineral supply and demand responsible for cyclical volatility is the substantial impact that changes in the overall level of economic activity have on the demand for most min-

Table 5-2. *United States Consumption of Selected Mineral Commodities, by End-Use Industry, 1973*
Percentage

| | | Industry | | | | |
|---|---|---|---|---|---|---|
| Mineral commodity | Appliance and equipment | Automo- bile and other transpor- tation | Con- struction | Electrical | Machinery | All other |
| Aluminum | 10 | 21 | 27 | 14 | 7 | 21 |
| Chromium | a | 18 | 23 | 3 | 15 | 41 |
| Copper | a | 8 | 14 | 61 | 10 | 7 |
| Iron and steel | 6 | 30 | 28 | a | 20 | 16 |
| Lead | a | 44 | 5 | 8 | a | 43 |
| Manganese | 4 | 22 | 21 | a | 15 | 38b |
| Nickel | 9 | 24 | 8 | 17 | 9 | 33 |
| Tin | a | 14 | 14 | 17 | 11 | 44 |
| Zinc | a | 22 | 32 | 11 | 9 | 26 |

Source: U.S. Bureau of Mines, *Minerals in the U.S. Economy* (GPO, 1975).
a. Consumption is small and included in *All other*.
b. Includes processing losses.

eral products. As a result, for most mineral products the demand curve shifts considerably over the business cycle.

One reason that the elasticity of demand for most mineral products with respect to income is very high in the short run is apparent from table 5-2, which shows the heavy use of mineral products in industries whose production is greatly affected by changes in the overall level of economic activity: appliance and equipment, automobile and other transportation, construction, electrical, and machinery. There are, of course, some mineral commodities whose use is not concentrated in these highly volatile industries. Potash, phosphate rock, and sulfur, for example, are largely consumed in the production of fertilizers, and their demand is far more stable over the business cycle. But these are exceptions.

If business cycles in the United States, Western Europe, and Japan become increasingly synchronized as their economies grow more integrated and interdependent, the instability of mineral markets could increase in severity. Figure 5-1 suggests some convergence in both the upswings and downswings of industrial production in the United States and in Europe and Japan, particularly since the late 1960s. Whether this will

Figure 5-1. *Annual Percentage Changes in Industrial Production,
United States and OECD European Countries and Japan, 1951–74*

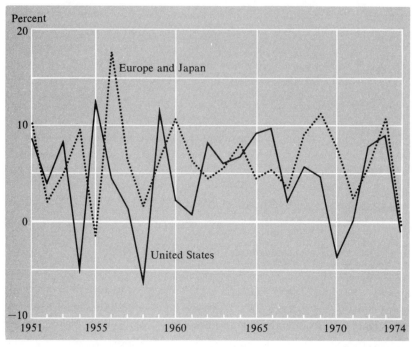

    Source: Richard N. Cooper and Robert Z. Lawrence, "The 1972–75 Commodity Boom," *Brookings Papers on Economic Activity, 3:1975,* p. 683.

continue in the future, of course, is uncertain. If it does, it will aggravate cyclical volatility, for when demand is weak in the United States it will be weak in other industrialized countries as well, leaving little opportunity for American producers to divert some of their surplus supplies abroad. Similarly, when demand is strong in the United States, it will be more difficult to relieve shortages by importing from abroad.

In addition to changes in the level of industrial production over the business cycle, several other factors periodically cause shifts in the supply or demand curve for mineral products and thereby contribute to cyclical volatility. One of the most intriguing and baffling of these is private speculation. One would expect speculators to buy when the price was low and sell when it was high, thereby making profits for themselves and at the same time stabilizing the price of mineral commodities over the business cycle. However, those with firsthand experience in the industry generally argue that speculation, including the inventory holdings of fabricators, tends to be destabilizing rather than stabilizing. In the words of Ronald Prain:

Generally speaking, when the market is oversupplied and copper is at a relatively low price, [fabricators] are seldom anxious to increase their stocks. In fact, during times of surplus they are often reluctant to continue to hold such stocks as they may have and will rely on being able to buy at fairly short notice. During a prolonged market depression fabricators will tend to reduce their inventories to a very low level and whilst this is in part a reflection of the fact that they are not fabricating and selling as much copper as before, it is also a reflection of their views of the whole supply position.

Copper fabricators, therefore, are apt to do most of their purchasing on a rising market and when, as in 1964, there is a sudden upturn after a long period of depressed prices, there will be a rush to buy metal, not only for current consumption but also for stockbuilding.

This elasticity of stocks in the hands of fabricators accounts for much of the aggravated swings in the copper market. When the market is weak it is doubly weak because copper is taken out of stock to be used in an already shrinking consumption. When the market is strong it is doubly so for additional supplies are sought, not only for actual consumption, but to build up stocks as well.[2]

There is other evidence, as well, suggesting that speculation is destabilizing in the mineral sector. Japan, as table 5-3 indicates, sharply increased its imports of many minerals during the boom period of 1973 and early 1974, apparently overreacting to fears of shortages. A significant portion of these imports exceeded the country's consumption requirements, and when mineral markets softened in mid-1974, Japan reduced its inventories of many materials by increasing its exports. This, of course, accentuated the downturn in these markets. Additional evidence that speculation tended to exacerbate the rise in commodity prices during 1973 and early 1974 is found in a recent study by Cooper and Lawrence.[3]

While empirical evidence exists suggesting that speculation has been destabilizing, the reasons for such perverse behavior are not entirely clear. While producers do tend to increase their stocks when demand is depressed and to draw on these stocks when it revives, they apparently are not willing to accumulate stocks sufficiently large to offset the behavior

2. Ronald Prain, *Copper: The Anatomy of an Industry* (London: Mining Journal Books, 1975), p. 133.
3. Richard N. Cooper and Robert Z. Lawrence, "The 1972–75 Commodity Boom," *Brookings Papers on Economic Activity, 3:1975.*

Table 5-3. *Japanese Trade in Selected Mineral Commodities, 1970–75*

| Mineral commodity | 1970 | 1971 | 1972 | 1973 | 1974 | 1975[a] |
|---|---|---|---|---|---|---|
| *Aluminum*[b] | | | | | | |
| Imports | 223 | 204 | 271 | 373 | 385 | 271 |
| Exports | 3 | 22 | 7 | 2 | 24 | 37 |
| *Copper*[b] | | | | | | |
| Imports | 302 | 268 | 294 | 395 | 293 | 210 |
| Exports | 47 | 11 | 26 | 27 | 280 | 31 |
| *Nickel*[b] | | | | | | |
| Imports | 10.1 | 8.3 | 12.0 | 14.3 | 16.3 | 7.8 |
| Exports | 0.4 | 0.2 | | 0.2 | 0.5 | 1.3 |
| *Magnesium*[b] | | | | | | |
| Imports | 2.1 | 0.7 | 2.9 | 6.0 | 12.7 | 1.9 |
| Exports | 0.1 | | | 0.1 | 1.4 | 2.6 |
| *Tungsten*[c] | | | | | | |
| Imports | 106.4 | 40.3 | 45.4 | 204.0 | 285.5 | 19.6 |
| Exports | 50.6 | 91.6 | 81.1 | 64.2 | 113.9 | 232.7 |
| *Molybdenum*[c] | | | | | | |
| Imports | 114.8 | 10.3 | 52.3 | 196.3 | 80.5 | 16.6 |
| Exports | 17.5 | 23.4 | 21.6 | 34.7 | 20.7 | 19.2 |
| *Tantalum*[c] | | | | | | |
| Imports | 20.8 | 11.0 | 13.7 | 24.1 | 34.5 | 16.0 |
| Exports | 2.3 | 0.9 | 2.3 | 0.5 | 25.3 | 15.0 |

Source: Edward R. Fried, "International Trade in Raw Materials: Myths and Realities," *Science* (February 20, 1976), p. 642.
a. Figures for 1975 are projections by the Japanese Ministry of Finance.
b. Measured in $10^3$ metric tons.
c. Measured in $10^3$ kg.

of fabricators and other speculators. There are at least two possible reasons for this. First, as pointed out in the last chapter, producers often encounter difficulties in raising large sums of capital when market conditions are depressed and their profits low. At some point, the financial burden of carrying increasingly large stocks limits this activity. Second, the existence of very large stocks tends to overhang the market and postpone the day when increased demand will permit a rise in price.

Even more difficult to explain is why independent speculators[4] do not introduce a greater degree of stability in mineral pricing. Apparently when markets are soft and prices are falling there is a tendency to wait for the price to fall even further, even though the current price is thought to

4. An independent speculator is neither a producer nor a consumer of the mineral commodity in which he speculates.

be well below the long-run market price. Similarly, when prices are rising, independent speculators tend to hold their stocks and even to add to them in anticipation of further short-run gains.

The destabilizing stockpiling behavior of fabricators is, to some extent, easier to understand, for they have other concerns besides earning speculative profits. In particular, they place a very high value on adequacy of supply, for the cost of running out of raw materials and being forced to curtail operations is great. Consequently, during periods of threatening shortages, fabricators try to build up their inventories even though the price of materials may seem unduly high. When the market is soft, however, they have no fear of a shortage. Since supplies can be acquired quickly from producers, fabricators have a tendency to reduce the size of their inventories.

While the preceding explanation for the perverse behavior of speculation is far from complete, and much more work is needed before this apparent market failure is fully understood, for the purposes of this study what is important is the fact that speculation appears to accentuate—at times severely—the short-run fluctuations in the mineral sector caused by the business cycle.

Another factor that may shift mineral supply and demand curves over the short run is the accumulation and disposal of government stockpiles. In the postwar period, a number of governments, particularly the United States, accumulated stockpiles of mineral commodities largely for strategic purposes. Some of these stocks were created and enlarged during periods of strong demand, thereby making short-run shortages even more severe. Other stocks, however, were accumulated when markets were soft or disposed of when demand was up and consequently tended to reduce short-run instability.[5]

The outbreak of war may also abruptly shift the demand curve for some mineral commodities. Nickel, for example, is heavily used in the production of high-grade steels needed for armaments. As a result, the demand for nickel jumped sharply during World War I, World War II, the Korean War, and the Vietnam War. After each of these conflicts, despite efforts by the industry to encourage the use of nickel in nonmilitary goods, demand fell sharply.

Finally, interruptions in the production of mineral commodities can

5. For an interesting discussion of the impact of U.S. stockpiling activity on the zinc market, see Barry A. Hillman, "Investment in the Zinc Industry 1950–1970" (Ph.D. dissertation, Pennsylvania State University, forthcoming), chap. 8.

shift supply curves. A prolonged strike against the major Canadian nickel firms in 1969, for example, greatly reduced the supply of nickel that year. Accidents at mining facilities can have a similar effect. The disastrous cave-in at the Mufulira Copper Mine in Zambia in September 1970 reduced that country's copper output to the lowest level since 1966. Wars and civil disruptions, such as occurred in Zaire shortly after that country acquired its independence from Belgium, can also adversely affect the available supply of mineral commodities. More recently, the Angolan civil war and the embargo against Rhodesia curtailed shipments of Zambian copper abroad.

## The Consequences of Shortages and Gluts

In the mineral sector, one finds basically two different types of markets, each of which deals with the cyclical volatility problem in a different way. The first are competitive markets, where prices are free to rise or fall to any level necessary to equate the available supply and demand. The second and more common are markets with administered or producers' prices. In these markets, the major firms are typically limited in number and consequently can exercise some control, at least in the short run, over prices.

### Competitive Markets

Copper, lead, zinc, tin, and silver are traded on the London Metal Exchange in competitive markets. Prices of these commodities are allowed to move to any level required to clear the market. Tungsten, gold, and ferrous and nonferrous scrap also are sold on competitive markets.

In these markets, the short-run supply curve is the marginal cost curve for the industry and looks like the supply curve shown in figure 5-2a. Until the constraining effects of existing capacity are reached, the extra or marginal costs of producing an additional unit of output remain constant or rise gradually, so that supply is quite responsive to minor increases in price. Once capacity is fully utilized, however, the supply curve turns sharply upward. Figure 5-2a also shows the demand for a mineral commodity at the peak of the business cycle ($D_p$), at the trough of the business cycle ($D_t$), and at the midpoint of the business cycle ($D_m$). Since the

Figure 5-2. *Nature of Mineral Supply and Demand in a Competitive Market and a Producer-Controlled Market: Consequences for Price and Output over the Business Cycle*

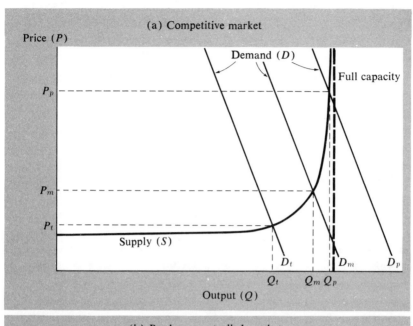

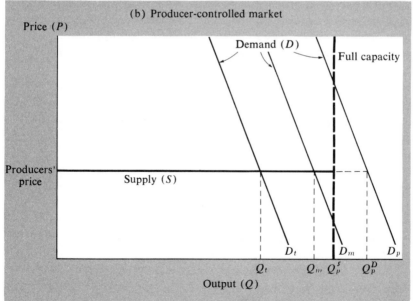

short-run elasticity of demand with respect to price is low, the slope of the demand curve is steep.

Production at the peak of the cycle $(Q_p)$ pushes on the limits of capacity, the price $(P_p)$ is high, and firms can generally earn large profits. At the trough of the cycle, the price $(P_t)$ is far lower and production $(Q_t)$ is curtailed so that considerable capacity is idle. Since firms have an incentive to continue to produce as long as the price covers their out-of-pocket or variable costs, the price at this stage of the business cycle does not allow most firms to recover their average total costs. Indeed, given the high fixed costs, which derive from the capital intensive nature of mineral production, price can fall far below average costs and losses can be substantial.

The ferrous scrap industry in the United States illustrates the instability of competitive markets over the business cycle. The production of purchased scrap rose from 49 to 56 to 60 million tons in 1972, 1973, and 1974, and then dropped to 45 million tons in 1975. Similarly, the average price per ton increased from $36.89 in 1972 to $57.95 in 1973 to $108.52 in 1974, and then fell to $72.72 in 1975.[6] Total revenues (and presumably profits) varied greatly, because when output was down so were prices. This occurred because the instability was generated by shifts in the demand curve.

When instability arises because of shifts in the supply curve, prices are up when output is down, and their combined impact on revenue earnings and profits is not as severe. (This is common for agricultural commodities, whose demand is relatively stable from year to year, but whose supply varies in response to weather conditions.) Unfortunately, the dominant source of instability for most mineral commodities arises from shifts in the demand curve, caused largely by fluctuations in industrial production and speculative activity. Producers of these commodities who operate in competitive markets experience rather large changes in profits over the short run. Indeed, even producers who do not sell in competitive markets are plagued by large swings in profits, as the next section indicates.

### Producer-Controlled Markets

Many mineral commodities, such as steel and aluminum, are sold by their producers at prices they set. In the United States, copper, lead, and

6. These and the following figures are from U.S. Bureau of Mines, *Commodity Data Summaries 1976* (USBM, January 1976), p. 86. Production is measured in short tons. Prices are for long tons of average No. 1 heavy melting composite scrap.

Figure 5-3. *Price of Copper, London Metal Exchange and U.S. Producers, 1966–76*

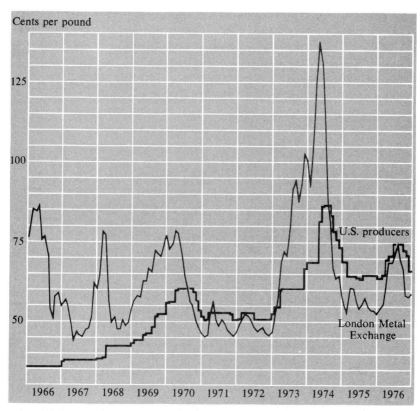

Sources: For 1966–73, U.S. Bureau of Mines, *Minerals Yearbook* (GPO, annual); for 1974–76, Bureau of Mines, "Mineral Industry Surveys: Copper Industry, Monthly" (December issues 1974–76).

zinc are also sold in producer-controlled markets, and at times the prices in these markets differ substantially from those on the London Metal Exchange or New York Commodity Exchange (see figure 5-3). Just how such differences persist for commodities that are traded internationally is an intriguing question. Part of the explanation appears to lie with the strong buyer-seller ties that exist between the large American nonferrous metal producers and their customers. In a sense, these ties are implicit long-term contracts. Consumers continue to buy from these firms when the free-market price falls below the producers' price, because they know if they do these producers will provide them with needed supplies at prices below those in the free market when supplies are tight.[7]

In producer-controlled markets, prices are set to reflect long-run conditions rather than short-run supply and demand. As a result, prices change less frequently than in competitive markets. This pricing behavior has led some to the conclusion that the firms in these industries are not competitive, that they tacitly collude to earn excess profits. This, however, is not necessarily the case. While such behavior does suggest that the major producers of a material do not compete via price among themselves, as a group they may actively compete for markets with the producers of substitute materials. As pointed out earlier, fabricators substitute one material for another on the basis of long-run—not short-run—changes in relative prices. Short-run fluctuations that do not reflect long-run trends are, from their point of view, disruptive and simply add to uncertainty. Thus, to penetrate new markets and protect those they already have, producers may keep long-run prices as low as costs—and the need for a rate of return sufficient to raise capital—will permit.

The supply curve in producer-controlled markets is basically a horizontal line at the existing producers' price, which continues until capacity constraints prevent firms from supplying more output. At this point, the supply curve stops (or becomes vertical), as shown in figure 5-2b. The figure implies that the price of mineral commodities sold in producer markets remains constant over the entire cycle. In practice, of course, this is rarely the case; producers tend to raise prices during the boom phase of the cycle and for some commodities, such as copper, reduce prices during the depressed phase of the cycle. Nevertheless, both the magnitude and the frequency of changes in price are far less in producer-controlled markets than in competitive markets, as shown in figure 5-3, which compares the London Metal Exchange price of copper with the U.S. producers' price.[8]

While producer-controlled markets dampen the large swings in price

---

7. Other factors may also contribute to the different prices found in some metal markets. See, for example, David L. McNicol, "The Two Price Systems in the Copper Industry," *The Bell Journal of Economics*, vol. 6, no. 1 (Spring 1975), pp. 50–73.

8. To some extent, however, the stability of the posted U.S. producers' price exaggerates the actual situation in the United States, since producers at times give discounts from the posted price. See George J. Stigler and James K. Kindahl, *The Behavior of Industrial Prices* (Columbia University Press for the National Bureau of Economic Research, 1970).

Table 5-4. *Prices, Return on Equity, Production, and Capacity Utilization in the American Steel Industry, 1950–74*

| Year | Price index,[a] finished steel products | Return on equity (percent) | Total production, raw steel (millions of tons) | Capacity utilization (percent) |
|------|------|------|------|------|
| 1950 | 63.2 | 14.3 | 97 | 97 |
| 1951 | 64.5 | 12.3 | 105.2 | 101 |
| 1952 | 67.5 | 8.5 | 93 | 86 |
| 1953 | 73.0 | 10.7 | 111.6 | 95 |
| 1954 | 74.7 | 8.1 | 88.3 | 71 |
| 1955 | 79.9 | 13.5 | 117.0 | 93 |
| 1956 | 87.2 | 12.7 | 115.2 | 90 |
| 1957 | 93.9 | 11.4 | 112.7 | 85 |
| 1958 | 96.5 | 7.2 | 85.3 | 61 |
| 1959 | 96.5 | 8.0 | 93.4 | 63 |
| 1960 | 96.1 | 7.2 | 99.3 | 67 |
| 1961 | 95.8 | 6.1 | 98.0 | 71 |
| 1962 | 95.6 | 5.4 | 98.3 | 70 |
| 1963 | 97.3 | 7.0 | 109.3 | 76 |
| 1964 | 96.8 | 8.8 | 127.1 | 88 |
| 1965 | 98.0 | 9.8 | 131.5 | 88 |
| 1966 | 99.4 | 10.2 | 134.1 | 88 |
| 1967 | 100.8 | 7.7 | 127.2 | 82 |
| 1968 | 103.1 | 7.6 | 131.5 | 85 |
| 1969 | 110.0 | 7.6 | 141.3 | 91 |
| 1970 | 116.6 | 4.3 | 131.5 | 86 |
| 1971 | 128.0 | 4.5 | 120.4 | 81 |
| 1972 | 130.2 | 6.0 | 133.2 | 85 |
| 1973 | 135.4 | 9.5 | 150.8 | 96 |
| 1974 | 192.0 | 16.7 | 145.7 | 94 |

Source: U.S. Council on Wage and Price Stability, *A Study of Steel Prices* (GPO, 1975), table 3-1.
a. Figures are for December of year; price index base is 1967 = 100.

over the business cycle, they are far less successful in reducing fluctuations in capacity utilization and profits. For example, as table 5-4 illustrates, prices in the American steel industry have risen in a persistent manner over the postwar period, while returns on equity and capacity utilization have moved in both directions and been far more volatile. In the aluminum industry, production in the United States exceeded 99 percent of capacity in 1974 and then dropped to only 77 percent in 1975.[9] In Canada production fell from 92 to 77 percent of capacity over these two years, and in Japan from 89 to 61 percent.

9. These and the following figures are based on data from U.S. Bureau of Mines, *Commodity Data Summaries 1976*, p. 5.

Since prices are maintained over the business cycle and since the short-run price elasticity of demand for most mineral products is low, the profits of firms operating in producer-controlled markets probably vary less over the cycle than those of firms in competitive markets. In competitive markets, profits are reduced during a downturn in economic activity by contractions in both output and price. Although output in producer-controlled markets may fall slightly more (since there is less of a decline in price and so less of a stimulus to demand), prices are maintained, and on balance, profits fall by smaller—though still substantial—amounts.

Producer-controlled markets differ from competitive markets in another important respect; namely, they do not, at all times, clear the market. During the peak of the business cycle, as illustrated in figure 5-2b, the available supply ($Q_p^s$) is not sufficient to satisfy the demand ($Q_p^D$). On such occasions, the major producers ration their output, usually favoring their traditional customers. They also tend to lengthen their delivery times. During the 1973–74 boom, shortages for some materials were so severe that companies resorted to bartering to keep their plants operating.[10] Conversely, during depressed market conditions, firms restrict output and accumulate stocks. In this regard, producer-controlled markets are similar to markets governed by international commodity agreements.

## Other Adverse Effects

Besides its immediate impact on prices, capacity utilization, profits, and shortages, cyclical volatility causes long-term adverse effects. Without funds for capital investment, mineral producers may delay additions to capacity and reduce exploration activity. This causes shortages three, four, or five years hence, and retards the discovery of new deposits.

Cyclical volatility also increases production costs above what they would otherwise be. This is in large part because these capital intensive industries do not use their capacity fully over the business cycle. Moreover, it is often expensive to close down and then reopen mines and mineral-processing facilities. Large furnaces, for example, often have to be relined with new bricks before they can be reactivated. In addition, operating costs may be increased, since training and other personnel costs are

10. For some interesting examples, see Ralph E. Winter, "Lending a Hand," *Wall Street Journal* (August 14, 1974), pp. 1–2.

likely to be higher as a result of the greater employee turnover. Finally, the uncertainty over the timing and level of profits entails a risk that investors must be compensated for. Therefore, mining facilities need a higher expected rate of return than would otherwise be the case to attract outside capital.

Host countries also suffer from cyclical volatility. Many of these countries depend heavily on domestic mineral production for taxes and foreign exchange earnings. Falling profits can seriously interrupt development plans by reducing taxes and foreign exchange earnings. In addition, since mineral firms may employ a number of nationals, unemployment can accompany a drop in production.

For consumers and the consuming countries, cyclical volatility creates problems particularly during the boom phase of the business cycle: sharply higher prices or rationing and extended delivery times. These developments may force fabricators to curtail production when demand is most pressing. Both price increases and bottlenecks tend to aggravate inflation at a time when inflationary pressure is strongest.

Finally, cyclical volatility may inhibit the recycling of scrap and the growth of secondary industries. Such industries tend to bear the brunt of depressed conditions. When demand is down, primary producers will continue to operate, at least in the competitive markets, as long as they are recovering their variable costs. While this is also true for secondary producers, their production technology tends to be more labor intensive and less capital intensive than primary production, and so their variable costs are higher. When prices fall, they are generally the first to cease production, even though their average total costs of production may be lower than those of the primary producers that remain in operation. Since it is costly to allow expensive equipment to remain idle, this is in a sense an efficient means of restricting overall production. Still, it does tend to stifle an industry that for other reasons society may want to promote.

# CHAPTER SIX

# Cartels and Embargoes

THE UNITED STATES, Western Europe, and Japan are the major consumers, outside the communist bloc, of nearly all mineral commodities. For geologic, economic, and political reasons, the production of most mineral products is also concentrated in just a few countries—though often not in the major consuming countries. Consequently, many mineral commodities enter international trade in substantial quantities at some stage of production. Thus, restrictions on the international movement of commodities can create regional shortages, even though the supply of mineral products worldwide may be more than adequate to meet demand.

Trade in mineral products may be interrupted or restricted for a number of reasons; strikes or war, for example, may disrupt rail or ocean transportation. However, since the 1973 Arab oil embargo and the sharp price increases unilaterally imposed by the Organization of Petroleum Exporting Countries (OPEC) shortly thereafter, most of the concern over shortages induced by trade constraints has focused on cartels, unilateral price actions by individual countries, and embargoes. The prospects and consequences of these types of actions are examined in this chapter.

## Cartels and Unilateral Actions[1]

Cartels are collusive agreements among producers to increase their monopoly profits or rents by such actions as fixing prices, dividing up

1. This section is an expanded version of John E. Tilton, "Cartels in Metal Indus-

markets, and restricting output. Cartels are not new to the mineral industries. For example, the history of the world copper and sulfur industries
before World War II is filled with attempts by major producing firms to
establish cartels and divide up markets.[2] What is new is the growing interest of host governments in following the OPEC example and in establishing producer associations and cartels.

Within the copper, bauxite, iron ore, mercury, and tungsten industries,
associations of major exporting countries have been formed over the last
few years. So far these organizations have not demonstrated an ability to
capture monopoly rents. The International Council of Copper Exporting
Countries, known by its French acronym as CIPEC, did try to restrict the
exports of member countries by 15 percent to help sustain the world price
of copper during the recent recession, but the results were not striking.
Indeed, the inability of the producing countries to sustain and stabilize the
price of copper has led the members of CIPEC to invite major consuming countries to join them in a producer-consumer organization, along the
lines of the International Tin Agreement. Nor have other producer associations been any more successful, though it is perhaps too early to judge
their effectiveness, since most were founded in 1974 or 1975.

Recent unilateral price actions by individual producing countries have
had a more dramatic impact, even though these actions appear to have
been motivated largely by the desire to take full advantage of the short-
term surge in demand that occurred during the 1973–74 boom rather than
the desire to obtain monopoly prices by restricting output. In 1974, for
example, Jamaica increased its bauxite taxes more than fivefold. Although
this was a unilateral action and not part of an agreement reached within
the International Bauxite Association (IBA), all the major bauxite producers in the IBA, with the exception of Australia, followed Jamaica's
lead and increased their taxes as well.

---

tries," *Earth and Mineral Sciences*, vol. 44, no. 6 (Pennsylvania State University,
March 1975), pp. 41–44.

2. See Orris C. Herfindahl, *Copper Costs and Prices: 1870–1957* (Johns Hopkins
University Press for Resources for the Future, 1959), chaps. 4 and 5; and Jared E.
Hazelton, *The Economics of the Sulfur Industry* (Johns Hopkins University Press
for Resources for the Future, 1970), chaps. 5 and 6. Fifty-one cartel agreements in
eighteen industries involved in international trade are identified in P. O. Eckbo,
*OPEC and the Experience of Previous International Commodity Cartels*, MIT
Energy Laboratory working paper 75-008WP (August 1975), cited in Charles J.
Johnson, "Cartels in Minerals and Metal Supply," *Mining Congress Journal*, vol. 62,
no. 1 (January 1976), p. 30.

In the fall of 1973, the Office Cherifien des Phosphates, the Moroccan government agency that runs the state owned phosphate monopoly, announced the first of a series of price increases that quadrupled the price of phosphate rock by the middle of 1974. Producers in the United States, which after Morocco is the second largest world exporter of phosphate rock, quickly followed Morocco's lead, though their price increases of 150 percent were somewhat more modest.[3]

The growing number of government sponsored producer associations and unilateral price increases imposed by host governments have raised the fear in many importing countries that, with increasing frequency, cartels run by producer governments will dictate the price and terms governing their access to vitally needed raw materials.

*Prospects*

The likelihood that the major producing countries of a particular mineral commodity can establish a cartel and maintain artificially high prices depends on (1) how large a share of the mineral's world exports, output, and reserves they control; (2) how little the demand falls as the price rises; (3) how little the supply from sources outside the cartel increases as the price rises; and (4) how strong the bonds among the countries are, which lend cohesion to a cartel and prevent members from cheating or leaving it.

SHARE OF EXPORTS, OUTPUT, AND RESERVES. For most minerals, the number of major producing and exporting countries is not great. As table 6-1 indicates, known reserves also tend to be concentrated in the major producing countries. Since the problems of organizing a cartel increase with the number of participants, this suggests that it should not be difficult to form cartels for many mineral commodities.

It is true that for some metals the primary producers' control over supply is diluted by secondary production. In 1975, for example, 23 percent of the copper and 47 percent of the lead consumed in the United States was produced from obsolete scrap.[4] In addition, industrialized countries are major producers of some mineral commodities. The United States, for

3. Ann Crittendon, "Phosphate: Taking a Leaf from Oil's Book," *New York Times,* November 9, 1975.
4. U.S. Bureau of Mines, *Commodity Data Summaries 1976* (GPO, 1976), pp. 46, 90.

Table 6-1. *Percentage of 1975 World Production and Reserves Shared by the Four Largest Producing Countries, Selected Mineral Commodities*

| Mineral commodity | Share of world production | Share of world reserves | Countries |
|---|---|---|---|
| Bauxite | 64 | 62 | Australia, Jamaica, Guinea, Surinam |
| Chromium[a] | 70 | 96 | Soviet Union, South Africa, Rhodesia, Philippines |
| Cobalt[b] | 90 | 64 | Zaire, Zambia, Canada, Morocco |
| Copper | 53 | 57 | United States, Chile, Canada, Soviet Union |
| Fluorspar | 51 | 42 | Mexico, Soviet Union, Spain, Thailand |
| Gold[b] | 84 | 88 | South Africa, Canada, United States, Australia |
| Iron ore | 55 | 61 | Soviet Union, Australia, United States, Brazil |
| Lead[b] | 59 | 77 | United States, Australia, Canada, Mexico |
| Manganese[b] | 78 | 95 | South Africa, Gabon, Brazil, Australia |
| Mercury | 65 | 65 | Spain, Soviet Union, China, Italy |
| Molybdenum[b] | 99 | 98 | United States, Canada, Chile, Peru |
| Nickel[b] | 63 | 65 | Canada, New Caledonia[c] |
| Phosphate rock[b] | 81 | 88 | United States, Morocco, Spanish Sahara, Tunisia |
| Platinum group | 99 | 99 | South Africa, Soviet Union, Canada[c] |
| Potash[b] | 90 | 95 | Canada, West Germany, United States, France |
| Silver | 53 | 60 | Peru, Mexico, Canada, United States |
| Tin | 65 | 48 | Malaysia, Soviet Union, Indonesia, Bolivia |
| Vanadium[a] | 85 | 96 | South Africa, United States, Soviet Union, Chile |
| Zinc | 43 | 57 | Canada, Australia, United States, Peru |

Source: Calculated from U.S. Bureau of Mines, *Commodity Data Summaries 1976* (GPO, 1976).
a. Figures are based on 1974 data.
b. Calculated for noncommunist countries only.
c. For nickel, figures are for two largest producers; for platinum for the three largest.

example, is the world's principal source of molybdenum. For others, such as chromium, a cartel would have to include countries in the Soviet bloc. For many mineral commodities, Canada, Australia, or South Africa are the major producers, countries sometimes considered unlikely to join producer cartels or to support monopoly increases in price. However, Australia, for example, has joined the bauxite, copper, and iron ore producer associations. Moreover, even if these countries do not formally participate in cartels, they may support their activities informally. As already pointed out, the American phosphate firms followed the lead of Morocco in raising prices in 1973 and 1974.

EFFECT OF PRICE ON DEMAND. The last chapter noted that, in the short run, price increases have little effect on the demand for most mineral products. This is because these products are used to produce other goods, and it takes time and money to change production processes. In the intermediate run and particularly in the long run, however, the demand for most mineral commodities is much more sensitive to changes in their own prices (see table 5-1) as well as to the price of substitutes.

EFFECT OF PRICE ON SUPPLY. Similarly, the responsiveness of mineral supplies outside the control of a cartel to increases in price tends to be low in the short run and high in the long run. This is largely because it takes several years for major new deposits to be developed, and even longer if townsites, harbors, and other such support facilities have to be built. There is, however, one important possible exception to this generalization. Over the postwar period, the United States has accumulated sizable strategic stockpiles, and for a number of mineral commodities, stocks appreciably exceed strategic requirements. Attempts by the major producers to set up cartels and to artificially raise prices for these commodities could provoke major disposals from the strategic stockpiles, which would constitute substantial short-run responses to increases in price.

COHESION AMONG PRODUCERS. In general, the cohesion of cartels in the mineral industries has been weak. Seldom have such efforts lasted for more than five years because either some members aspired to increase their world market share; or new producers, encouraged by high prices, entered the industry; or falling demand lured some producers into cutting prices in an attempt to avoid production cutbacks or large stockpile accumulations. In the past, however, most cartel activity has been carried out by private firms, while today host governments are the principal instigators. This could strengthen the durability of cartels, though for several reasons, maintaining the internal cohesion of mineral cartels is still likely to be difficult.

Many of the major producers depend heavily on mineral exports for tax revenues and foreign exchange earnings. To the extent that a cartel maintains price considerably above cost, the temptation to cheat will be great. The tin industry provides a recent illustration of this problem. During the first nine months of 1975, Burma reportedly exported some 3,000 tons of tin, while the country estimated its tin production for the entire year at about 600 tons. The unexplained exports apparently were Thai tin smuggled into Burma and then to international markets.[5] While Thailand is a

5. See Martyn Chase, "Detailed Reports of Tin Smuggling Arouse Intense Interest in London," *American Metal Market,* vol. 83, no. 40 (February 27, 1976), p. 6.

member of the International Tin Council and thus subject to export controls, Burma is not.

Disagreements over market shares and the evolution of these shares over time may also undermine cartels (or even prevent their formation). Countries with large undeveloped reserves, such as Peru, that hope to increase their mineral exports to stimulate domestic development are unlikely to adhere to cartel agreements that thwart such aspirations. And established producers may not be willing to accommodate plans that would result in a decline in their own share of world markets.

There is another factor that may strain the internal cohesion of cartels. Mineral production involves high fixed costs that continue whether production takes place or not. This, coupled with the fact that mineral production in many countries is an important source of government revenue, foreign exchange, sales for domestic support industries, and employment, means that during downswings in the business cycle, pressure mounts to cut price—either covertly or overtly—in the hope of keeping production and capacity utilization from falling too drastically. This is particularly true for countries that have little or no excess reserves of foreign exchange to cushion the impact of the downturn.

It is not true, however, as some have argued, that poor countries with small reserves will not participate in cartels because they cannot afford to withhold mineral exports from the market. Since the elasticity of demand for mineral products in the short run is low, withholding supplies increases total revenue and profits. Thus, a poor country could actually improve its financial position by withholding supply. This would work, of course, if, and only if, other producers would do the same.

Ideological differences among governments, it has been said, make it difficult for them to establish and maintain cartels. And the governments of the producing countries of many minerals do have conflicting political ideologies. The major producers of chromium, for example, are South Africa, the Soviet Union, Turkey, Rhodesia, and the Philippines. The major suppliers of manganese are the Soviet Union, South Africa, Brazil, Gabon, and India. Despite the intuitive appeal of this argument, however, experience suggests that the importance of such differences can easily be exaggerated. The Soviet Union, for example, has cooperated with South African interests to maintain the diamond cartel, since to do so was in its own interest. Similarly, despite its ideological commitment to free markets, the United States under the Webb-Pomerene Act allows its mineral producers to participate in cartels as long as only foreign markets are affected. In short, if the opportunities to earn monopoly profits are great, the incentives to cooperate will be strong regardless of ideological consideration. Moreover, as has already been noted, countries can both support cartels and benefit from their actions without formally participating.

As this review suggests, cartels of producing countries might succeed for at least a few years, since increases in price have little effect in the short run on either the demand or the supply of many minerals. Over the long run, however, the price elasticity of demand and supply tends to be high. Consequently, even if the cohesion of a cartel were maintained, members would find the demand for their exports falling over time as producers outside the cartel increased their production and consumers switched to alternative materials. Eventually, the cartel would have to abandon its artificially high price or lose its markets entirely.

Unilateral price actions are simpler to achieve than price actions by cartels. It is true that individual countries do not dominate to the necessary extent the exports, production, and reserves of as many minerals as do the top four or five producing countries. Still, for some minerals unilateral price raises are possible, particularly when demand is strong, as events in the bauxite and phosphate rock industries demonstrate. As with actions by cartels, such unilateral actions can succeed over the short run, but over the long run they are undermined by the same factors that undermine cartels. Already the unilateral price actions in phosphate rock and bauxite have encountered difficulties, though in both cases the loss in markets over the long run was greatly accelerated by the recession of 1975.[6]

The long-run adverse consequences of both cartel and unilateral price actions have led many to the conclusion that other mineral-producing countries will not follow the examples set by OPEC, Jamaica, and Morocco. This conventional wisdom, however, assumes that public officials in the producing countries are convinced of the long-term dangers and always act in their country's long-run interests. Both of these assumptions can be questioned.

First, policy makers in many exporting countries, including Canada

6. See, for example, Bob Regan, "Jamaica Hit Hard by U.S. Cut in Bauxite, Alumina Imports," *American Metal Market,* vol. 82, no. 236 (December 5, 1975), p. 8; and "Phosphate Rock: Production Down 4% in 1975," *Phosphorus & Potassium* (February 1976), pp. 5–7.

and Australia, are under increasing political pressure to extract more revenues from their mineral sector. In some cases, pressure is generated by a popular feeling that the country's natural resources for too long have been exploited by foreign firms without adequate payment to the host country. This attitude may be exacerbated by hostility toward foreign investment in general. In addition, some countries have pressing domestic needs and the mineral sector appears as the one possible source of additional funds for coping with these needs. Finally, the example of OPEC and the rhetoric in the United Nations regarding the new international economic order have increased the pressure to raise mineral prices. Thus, public opinion may force government officials to take such actions even when they are not in the long-run interest of their country.

Second, public officials may be more concerned about the short run than the long run because their job security may depend on visible signs of progress within a period of several years. Since supply and demand for mineral commodities is unresponsive to increase in price in the short run, a cartel or unilateral price action may produce substantial monopoly rents for at least several years. The price action seems to work. Its instigators are praised. By the time the adverse consequences become apparent, new public officials may be in office. Moreover, if a cartel or unilateral price action collapses—the likely outcome—its demise can be publicly mourned and blamed on other countries.

In addition, if the short run is long enough, the welfare of a country may well be best served, even over the long run, by joining a cartel or by instigating a unilateral price action. Although the long-run viability of its mineral sector is undermined, the excess profits earned over the short run can be used for education, public health, and capital investment, and the country may be better off even after the cartel collapses.

Third, officials do not possess perfect information. Neither they nor anyone else know with accuracy how much outside supply increases and demand decreases as price rises and how these responses increase with time. Much uncertainty also exists over future changes in the price of substitute materials. The adverse consequences for the producing countries of a copper cartel, for example, are likely to be less severe and take longer to occur if a strong bauxite cartel develops.

Similarly, forecasts of mineral demand vary widely, based as they are on different assumptions about future population, per capita income growth, and the intensity of mineral use at various income levels. Yet all this information is necessary to assess how soon after forming a cartel the adverse effects will develop and how severe they will be.

Fourth, in many mineral exporting countries, there is widespread concern that natural resources are being exploited too rapidly. Many argue that raw material wealth is a national legacy that should be conserved, perhaps for the day when the host country itself will be industrialized and in need of such materials. Proponents of this position stress high per unit profits for mineral resource operations rather than large total profits. They tend to overlook or discount the possibility that high taxes or cartelization may reduce a country's mineral production below the level that contributes most to the country's development and the future welfare of its people.

These factors all suggest that despite the long-run consequences for their mineral sector, the major exporting countries of at least some minerals may establish cartels or carry out unilateral actions in an attempt to extract monopoly rents. Though these efforts are likely to be short-lived, they can in some cases succeed for several years, since it takes that long to develop new supplies and change production processes to alternative materials.

### Consequences

The potential consequences of nonfuel mineral cartels, although small compared to OPEC's, are not trivial, even assuming they collapse within a few years. The monopoly profits earned at the expense of consumers can be substantial in the short run. For example, the additional profits earned by phosphate rock producers in 1974 as a result of the sharp price increases ran into the billions of dollars.[7] Moreover, since cartels tend to fall apart after several years, they may contribute to the short-run instability of mineral supplies and prices and thus aggravate the problems caused by cyclical volatility.

Perhaps more important, such efforts are likely to encourage mining corporations to turn to safer but higher-cost deposits outside the cartel. This is partly to reduce the risk of losing their capital investment. But in addition, since mineral production requires large capital investment, the corporations need access to raw material supplies that are secure and competitively priced, so that expensive facilities do not sit idle.

7. Crittendon, "Phosphate: Taking a Leaf from Oil's Book."

Finally, high prices and monopolistic control distort the rate and direction of technological change. During the time that substantial reserves of a mineral are controlled by a cartel, the research and development of that mineral's users are directed toward finding substitutes, new sources of supply, and improved conservation techniques. The best present-day example is among petroleum users. Another example is the aluminum industry, which is trying to develop the technology for producing aluminum from nonbauxite ores. Such distortion diminishes the efficiency of resource allocation in the major importing countries, but it is potentially more damaging to the exporting countries, since it may irrevocably reduce long-run demand for their minerals.

## Embargoes

Embargoes are another type of constraint on the international movement of minerals that may create regional shortages. Countries impose embargoes in response to either domestic or foreign conditions. In the latter case, the embargo is designed to harm, discipline, or influence the behavior of foreign countries. The Arab states, for example, imposed their oil embargo in 1973 to pressure the industrial countries to change their Middle East policies. Embargoes may be placed on imports as well as exports. The United Nations, for example, has sponsored an embargo against Rhodesian chromium and other products. Similarly, the United States has prohibited trade with Cuba.

Not all embargoes, however, are designed to effect changes in the policies of other states; some are imposed simply for domestic reasons. In 1973, for example, the United States restricted soybean exports in response to domestic pressure created by rising agricultural prices. And on a number of occasions, it imposed quotas on the export of ferrous and nonferrous scrap, often largely because of political pressure from secondary producers who were concerned over rising scrap prices and possible domestic shortages.

The prospects for embargoes in the future depend to some extent on their objectives. Those restrictions on trade that a country may impose for domestic reasons depend on internal political interests and any adverse foreign reactions. In the case of U.S. scrap iron exports, for example, domestic scrap producers oppose export controls, since controls reduce the price they receive. When the price of scrap rises sharply, however, their opposition to controls may be overwhelmed by domestic steel producers.

Embargoes have been imposed from time to time throughout history and presumably will continue to be imposed in the future. The growing involvement of governments in the mineral sector raises the possibility of more frequent and subtle uses of embargoes. During times of steel shortages, for example, governments with nationalized steel companies may encourage these companies to give preference to domestic customers.

Where the aim is to alter the policies of a foreign country, the use of embargoes is more limited for two reasons. First, for most nonfuel minerals the overall damage an embargo can inflict is small. Second, alternative sources of supply are often available. In the short run, other suppliers may have excess capacity, or the country itself may hold stocks that it can draw on. In the longer run, new sources of supply can be developed. Shortly after the end of World War II, for example, the Soviet Union cut off shipments of manganese to the United States. Although manganese is essential in steel production, the effects on the United States were minimal. The most significant consequence was that the United States developed new sources of supply in India and elsewhere.

Nevertheless, embargoes can in some instances be disruptive in the short run, especially for particular industries. Although such short-run effects can be alleviated over the long run, these responses do alter the investment pattern in a way that increases reliance on high-cost materials and suppliers. So the cost of embargoes both in the short and long run may not be negligible.

# CHAPTER SEVEN

# Shortages and Public Policy

MINERALS ARE THE FOUNDATION on which the industrial societies of Japan, Western Europe, and the United States are built. Although mineral production and processing do not constitute a large part of their national income, their high standard of living would be seriously threatened if the flow of minerals into their economies were cut off.

Mineral shortages manifest themselves in different ways. Supplies that are inadequate to satisfy demand at prevailing prices may be reflected in rationing, bartering, and delays in delivery. Alternatively, shortages may cause prices to rise rapidly, constraining demand and causing dislocation and hardship as traditional users are forced out of the market.

## The Prospects for Shortages

Chapter one points out that future mineral shortages could arise from several causes: depletion of mineral resources, inadequacy of investment, cyclical volatility, and interruptions or constraints on trade. Subsequent chapters examine each of these threats to the availability of mineral products.

Although the world will never run out of mineral deposits, depletion could, over time, substantially raise the cost of finding and processing minerals as man is forced to use deposits that are lower grade, more remote, and more difficult to process. This, in turn, could force up the real prices of mineral commodities. The evidence indicates that this will not be a problem for at least the remainder of this century. Moreover, depletion may not be a problem even in the next century or for that matter in the next millennium. While the tendency to exploit poorer deposits will tend to push costs up, technological change will have the opposite effect. Thus, over the long run, depletion will pose a serious problem only if the race between the cost-decreasing effects of new technology and the cost-increasing effects of depletion is won by the latter. The outcome of this race, which at this time cannot be foreseen, will depend not only on the pace of new technology but also on the rate of population growth and per capita mineral consumption around the world.

Insufficient expansion in production capacity could create more immediate shortages. And the capital necessary for expansion may not be available for several reasons. First, there could simply be overall capital shortages. Second, during depressed economic conditions profits are low or negative, and investment capital for new capacity is hard to raise. Third, during periods of rapid inflation, with rising construction costs and interest rates, an economically viable project requires abnormally high mineral prices, making it appear to be an unattracive investment. Fourth, boom conditions can bring on price controls. To attract new investment capital, there must be an adequate rate of profit over the entire business cycle; and since the profits of mineral firms are often low during economic recessions, they must be high during boom conditions.

The conflict over economic rents and host government participation does not appear to have significantly curtailed the overall level of investment in the mineral sector. However, it has altered the geographic location of new capacity and, by shifting exploration and development of new mineral projects away from a number of low-cost areas, has increased costs. In addition, it has retarded the economic development of host countries whose mineral industries have been curtailed, most of which are developing countries in need of growth. In the future the shift to high-cost areas may be offset by the environmental movement in the United States and other industrialized countries, by innovative techniques for spreading the risks and capital costs of new projects in developing countries, and by the growing role of host governments in investment decisions.

Shortages may also arise as a result of cyclical volatility. Here, short-run shifts in the demand or the supply curves create temporary shortages simply because neither supply nor demand responds quickly to changes in price. Because many mineral products are used largely in construction, capital goods, consumer durables, and transportation, demand is highly sensitive to the overall level of business activity. Shortages frequently arise during economic booms, followed by gluts during economic recessions. Cyclical volatility has been a problem in the past and could become more serious if the growing integration of the economies of the industrial countries increases the synchronization of their business cycles.

Finally, shortages can arise as a result of constraints on the international movement of mineral commodities. In this regard, cartels, unilateral price actions, and embargoes could create problems, at least for importing countries. While such shortages are unlikely to last more than several years, they can be costly to consumers and create significant dislocation in the short run.

In the light of these threats to the future adequacy of mineral commodities, the remainder of this chapter examines possible public policies for reducing the likelihood that shortages will arise and for mitigating their impact if they do.

## Macroeconomic Stabilization Policies

Macroeconomic stabilization policies have a great effect on the adequacy of mineral commodities, given that fluctuations in the business cycle are largely responsible for the cyclical volatility that plagues many mineral industries. Boom conditions create temporary though often severe shortages. Furthermore, inflation, price controls, and budget deficits have an effect on the availability of capital. However, it is difficult to be sanguine about the effectiveness of policy in reducing the size of business cycles and preventing long-run price rises. Even though economic knowledge in this area is advancing, achieving full employment and stable prices over the short and the long term is proving far more difficult than many had once thought.

Although a fluctuating business cycle is not likely to disappear soon, certain adverse aspects of macroeconomic policy could be corrected with changes in policy. One example is the periodic imposition of price controls on steel and other industries in the mineral sector. As long as there are fluctuations in the business cycle and as long as the profits of these industries are highly sensitive to such fluctuations, they will have to earn excessive profits during the boom phase of the cycle if, over the whole cycle, they are to realize a rate of profit that will attract the capital needed for future expansion. In this regard, pressure by the U.S. government on producers to lower prices during depressed economic conditions is likely to be counterproductive.[1] If it successfully lowers prices, the prices and profits required during the boom phase simply escalate, aggravating inflation when inflationary pressures are most severe. Moreover, controlled prices during the boom phase stifle new investment, and shortages will arise unless the government provides financial or other assistance.

The preceding discussion suggests that prices that do not change over the business cycle in response to short-run supply-and-demand conditions may facilitate macroeconomic stability. There is, of course, always the danger that when the underlying market structure permits such pricing, firms will not attempt to track the long-run market clearing price but rather restrict output, raise prices, and garner monopoly profits. However, as noted in the discussion on producer cartels, this is difficult to do over the long run unless established producers are protected from material substitution, new domestic suppliers, imports, and new resource-saving technology. Where the long-run elasticities of demand and supply are high with respect to price, as is the case for most mineral commodities, established producers are forced to compete even though industry concentration may be high and competition within the industry weak. Competitive pressure tends to discipline the major mineral firms, forcing them either to produce efficiently and to set prices that reflect competitive long-run conditions or to lose their markets to firms that do.

Finally, if large government budget deficits create an overall capital shortage, the consequences could be severe for the mineral sector because of its large capital requirements and high risk.

## Economic Stockpiles

Macroeconomic policies cannot eliminate the shortages caused by cyclical volatility, both because these policies are not likely to eliminate business fluctuations and because other factors shift the demand or supply

1. "Prices of Zinc are Under Study in Antitrust Case," *Wall Street Journal*, May 18, 1976.

curves of minerals. Another possible policy for alleviating this problem entails the creation of economic stockpiles. Historically, the United States has held strategic stockpiles to ensure an adequate supply of essential mineral materials in the event of war. At times, these stockpiles have been used to stimulate the development of domestic mineral industries, to cushion the adverse effects of imports, to alleviate depressed market conditions, and to meet other economic objectives. Still, strategic considerations have inhibited the use of these stockpiles for economic purposes, which has generated some interest within the U.S. government in the possibility of creating economic stockpiles.

A similar interest is found in Japan and Western Europe as well.[2] After several years of deliberation, the Japanese government in early 1976 approved 30 billion yen (about $100 million) for economic stockpiles of copper, aluminum, lead, and zinc.[3] In 1972 the French government decided in principle to establish economic stockpiles, though only in 1975 were significant funds appropriated. For a number of years, through the use of unusual fiscal policies governing inventory write-offs and other aspects of corporate taxation, Sweden has encouraged firms to hold economic stockpiles.

The recent interest in economic stockpiles raises the question of just how effective they might be in alleviating the adverse consequences of cyclical volatility. Chapter five points out that these consequences vary with the nature of the market. In competitive markets, the major problems are (1) sharp fluctuations in prices and (2) underutilization of capacity when the market is depressed. In theory at least, the government could greatly reduce the severity of both of these problems by accumulating stocks when prices were low and then releasing them when prices were high. This would supplement the demand when the market was weak, raising prices and stimulating production and capacity utilization. When the market was tight, it would supplement supply and reduce prices. Since mineral production is capital intensive, a government stockpile program that improved capacity utilization would reduce costs. It would also alleviate inflationary pressures when they are likely to be strongest. Finally, it would enhance the efficiency with which mineral supplies are

2. See, for example, U.S. Office of Technology Assessment, *An Assessment of Alternative Economic Stockpiling Policies,* OTA-M-36 (GPO, 1976), pp. 36–37.

3. John Hataye, "Japanese Begin to Allot Funds for Nonferrous Stockpiling Program," *American Metal Market,* vol. 83, no. 31 (February 13, 1976), pp. 1, 20.

allocated over time by restricting low-priority use (as measured by willingness to pay) during recession and increasing high-priority use during economic booms.

In producer-controlled markets, the major problems created by cyclical volatility are (1) physical shortages requiring rationing and long delays in delivery when the economy is booming and (2) underutilization of capacity during depressed market conditions. Here again, the government in theory could reduce these problems by economic stockpiling. Accumulating stocks when production would otherwise be low would stimulate capacity utilization. When shortages arise these stocks could be disposed of, augmenting the available supply. As with competitive markets, a stockpiling program could not only reduce the periodic shortages caused by cyclical volatility but also reduce average production costs and enhance the allocation of mineral products to the highest priority uses.

There are reservations about the desirability of government-run buffer stocks. Some of the reservations raise legitimate concerns, but others are based on misconceptions:

1. *Since private speculators are motivated to buy when the price is low and sell when the price is high, they will assure that the private sector holds the optimal amount of stocks over the business cycle, thus stabilizing prices and production.* Although the reasons are not completely understood, evidence exists indicating that speculation tends to be destabilizing rather than stabilizing (see chapter five). If the private market does fail in this regard, some form of government intervention may be desirable.

2. *Stockpiles overhang the market, dampening demand, depressing prices, and discouraging investment.* This contention raises the question of how stockpiles maintained without increase or decrease in size could affect supply and demand, which determine price. Stockpiles may alter investor expectations, thereby discouraging investment and restricting supply; but this would raise prices, not lower them. Stockpiles are unlikely to change significantly the end-use demand of most mineral products, since this demand is derived from the demand for final goods and depends primarily on overall economic conditions and consumers' tastes. Of course, the existence of large stocks and the realization that they will be released in time of shortages would reduce the demand of speculators and fabricators when markets were tight, prices were rising, and shortages were threatening. But this phenomenon would be stabilizing, for increases in

private stocks acquired during tight markets are typically drawn down once prices begin to fall, accelerating the decline.

3. *Price changes are desirable because they provide important signals for decisions on investment, material substitution, material research and development, and the allocation of mineral supplies.* This, of course, is true, and no economic stockpile should attempt to keep prices at a fixed level indefinitely. Rather, the objective should be to dampen or eliminate short-run fluctuation around the long-run market-clearing trend. Indeed, attempts to do otherwise are likely to fail. If the price is maintained above the long-run market-clearing level, the stockpile size must be increased indefinitely. If the price is set below the long-run market-clearing level, the available stocks are depleted eventually, and the artificially low price can no longer be maintained—an effect aptly illustrated by the attempt in the early 1970s to maintain the price of gold at $35 an ounce.

While changes in prices along the long-run trend are desirable and provide important signals for investment and material substitution, severe short-run fluctuations around this trend are neither necessary nor desirable. Investment, material substitution, and research and development decisions should be made on the basis of long-run—not short-run—price trends. Short-run price fluctuations could serve to allocate temporarily limited supplies to their highest priority uses, but such a shortage would be eliminated with an economic stockpile.

4. *Economic stockpiles have never worked; for example, buffer stocks under the International Tin Agreement failed to keep prices within prescribed boundaries.* How tin prices would have fluctuated in the absence of tin stockpiles is unknown; conceivably, the variation could have been more severe. Moreover, the tin buffer stock operated, at times, under the disadvantages of being too small and of having to keep tin prices within an unrealistic range. United States' stockpiles of agricultural commodities succeeded for years in protecting the world against crop failures and the sharp price increases that crop failures cause. In any case, even if the record were clear regarding the past performance of buffer stocks, to assume simply because they have not worked in the past that they cannot be made to work in the future seems unduly pessimistic.

5. *Governments are incapable of determining and tracking the long-run market-clearing price, and mistakes foster inappropriate investment decisions and, eventually, either severe gluts or shortages. In addition, governments may abuse economic stockpiles and use them for inappropriate*

*purposes, such as threatening to release them to prevent firms from rais-ing prices.* The potential for both inept and malicious actions on the part of government stockpile managers does exist as long as they have discretionary authority over when stocks are accumulated and disposed of. Legislation setting up a buffer stock scheme could temper the authority of the manager, stipulating that stocks must be accumulated at a fixed rate once the price dropped 10 percent below some specified level and must be disposed of at a fixed rate once the price climbed to 10 percent above the specified level. During periods of accumulation, each time the funds available for stockpile purchases fell by 10 percent, the specified price level could be decreased by a certain percentage. Similarly, during periods of disposal, each time the available stockpile fell by 10 percent the specified price could be increased. Such a procedure would ensure that the floor and ceiling prices would change over time in response to changes in the long-run market-clearing price. At the same time, short-run fluctuations around the trend would be dampened, though not completely eliminated.[4]

6. *The costs of stockpiling are simply too high to warrant their use for stabilization purposes. To accumulate, for example, an adequate buffer stock of copper, even if purchased when prices were relatively depressed, would entail an expenditure of several billion dollars.*[5] This position tends to confuse the acquisition costs with the real costs of stockpiling, which are the resources actually consumed in acquiring, maintaining, and disposing of stocks. The distinction between the two costs is crucial, for acquisition costs merely represent the exchange of one type of asset (money) for another (commodities). Like the individual who draws down his bank account to invest in corporate bonds, a government that purchases commodities for a public stockpile is no poorer after the transaction than before. The composition of its portfolio has changed, but the total value of its assets remains the same. The expenditure of hundreds of millions or even billions of dollars for a large stockpile can, of course, create problems and inhibit the creation of a stockpiling program, but it does not represent a drain on the real resources of society.

Even the real costs of establishing and operating a buffer stock may

4. L. St. Clare Grondona has for years advocated a stockpiling program that is in some ways similar to the one described here. See his *Economic Stability is Attainable* (London: Hutchinson Benham, 1975).

5. See William E. Hoffman, "Asarco Exec Calls Hope Slim for Int'l Copper Price Accord," *American Metal Market,* vol. 83, no. 65 (April 2, 1976), p. 2.

be not a drain but an asset, since the operation could realize a profit: stocks are acquired when the market is depressed and prices are low and released when the market is tight and prices are high. The capital gains earned in the process of turning over stocks may be more than adequate to offset the interest and other costs incurred in operating the program.

Among the real costs of stockpiling are the opportunity cost, or interest charges, on the capital used to purchase commodities. The manpower and facilities required to manage and store stockpiles, along with any deterioration in quality or theft that occurs while stocks are held, must also be counted as part of the real cost, though for most mineral products these costs are small compared to the interest charges. While the appropriate interest rate that should be used in assessing possible government projects is open to dispute, in real terms it probably lies between 3 percent and 10 percent. This implies that the real annual costs of stockpiling are far less than the acquisition costs. From society's point of view, the acquisition costs constitute a financing problem that the government should resolve one way or another if the benefits to society of a stockpiling program are expected to exceed its real costs. This is true regardless of the magnitude of the real costs.

Upon careful examination, many of the reservations regarding economic stockpiles are simply not valid. A few do raise legitimate concerns, but even in these cases there appear to be promising avenues for circumventing the problems. In light of the potential benefits, economic stockpiles for stabilization purposes are worthy of serious consideration.

In addition to alleviating shortages arising from cyclical volatility, they can also be used to counteract shortages induced by cartels, unilateral actions, and embargoes. If stockpiles were available in consuming countries, export restrictions by producing countries would simply reduce their profits, foreign exchange earnings, and employment benefits, and though the stockpiles would eventually be depleted, exporters would face a year or two of depressed conditions in a major sector of their economies. In view of the short time horizon of most public officials, this would be a sizable deterrent to export restrictions. Moreover, a stockpile sufficient to last for several years would provide time for the development of new sources of supply and the substitution of alternative materials, which would cushion the impact of a shortage during the most acute adjustment period.

### International Commodity Agreements

Along with the interest in economic stockpiles, increasing attention is being focused on international commodity agreements, which are basically associations of the major importing and exporting states. Such associations attempt to regulate prices of primary products through the use of buffer stocks, production or export controls, and other means, in accordance with agreed upon principles. Commodity agreements are not new; they have existed over the postwar period in wheat, sugar, cocoa, coffee, tin, and a few other commodities. What is new is the enthusiasm with which they are now being advocated for a host of critical materials, primarily by the developing countries through the United Nations Conference on Trade and Development.

Two benefits claimed for international commodity agreements are of particular interest with regard to alleviating possible mineral shortages. First, through the use of buffer stocks and export controls, commodity agreements may reduce the adverse effects of cyclical volatility. Second, by providing a forum at which exporting and importing countries can resolve their differences, commodity agreements may diminish the probability of unilateral actions and producer cartels.

One might have reservations about the ability of an international organization to track the long-run market-clearing trend and about the possible misuse of stockpiles. These objections, however, could presumably be overcome by adoption of an automatic stockpiling procedure that left no discretion in the hands of stockpile managers. Moreover, there may be advantages to having buffer stocks run by a number of countries through an international accord, rather than by individual states. A cooperative international effort could have political benefits. Also, if price fluctuations are stabilized to such an extent that capital gains earned on the turnover of stocks do not cover the costs of operating the stockpile, an international agreement could distribute the financial burden.

Whether commodity agreements would significantly reduce the likelihood of producer cartels appears more doubtful. Presumably, producers would forgo the expected benefits of cartelization only if the benefits of joining a commodity agreement were as large or larger. This suggests that commodity agreements might have to stabilize prices above their long-run market-clearing levels, an action that, in the long run, may destroy markets, given the opportunities to develop alternative sources of supply or to use alternative materials for most mineral commodities. Thus, though many producing countries see commodity agreements as a means of achieving a transfer of real income from consuming to producing countries—by setting prices at what they see as just levels—commodity agreements would not serve either importing countries or exporting countries if used this way. It must be remembered, too, that many of the world's poorest nations are net importers of mineral commodities, and a number of wealthy countries, such as Canada, Australia, and South Africa, are major exporters of mineral commodities.

## Other International Accords

There are other types of international accords besides commodity agreements that conceivably could reduce the likelihood of future mineral shortages. Two possibilities are regulations governing international trade and international ground rules for foreign investment.

Over the postwar period, under the auspices of the General Agreement on Tariffs and Trade (GATT), many countries lowered their tariff and nontariff barriers to imports and agreed not to increase restrictions on imports unilaterally, except under certain circumstances. While international arrangements have formalized the rules governing access to markets and have made it easier for exporting countries to penetrate foreign markets, no parallel movement has been undertaken by importing countries with regard to access to raw materials. Over most of the postwar period, access to raw materials was not a problem. Industrial countries and other states could obtain primary products throughout most of the world without restrictions and often at declining real prices.

The growing interest in producer cartels and the increasing incidence of export controls, however, suggest that institutional arrangements guaranteeing access to raw materials on a competitive basis may now be needed.[6] New regulations, for example, might stipulate that countries that engage in embargoes or restrict output so as to set monopoly prices could

6. Recent negotiations conducted under the auspices of the General Agreement on Tariffs and Trade considered regulations covering access to raw material markets. See Tom Walsh, "Industrial Nations Seek to Assure Raw Materials Access Within Gatt," *American Metal Market*, vol. 82, no. 219 (November 10, 1976), p. 3.

lose their most-favored-nation preferences in other areas of trade. If discriminatory tariffs were placed on some of their exports, internal political pressure would mobilize against an embargo or the cartel.

One might ask why the major exporters of mineral commodities would agree to such an arrangement, since it would appear that they are giving up certain rights. But even the major primary product exporters would benefit from such an arrangement, for no country is totally self-sufficient in mineral resources. In addition, mineral producers aspiring to diversify into manufacturing industries would now have more negotiating power. In exchange for assuring the industrial nations equal access to their raw material supplies, mineral producing countries could negotiate lower tariffs for industries in which they have a comparative advantage. Often such industries are depressed or declining in developed nations and are therefore highly protected. The shoe and textile industries are classic examples. Also, many of the industrial states have very low tariffs on unprocessed primary products and significantly higher tariffs on the more processed intermediate products. As a result, the effective level of protection for many refined and fabricated mineral products substantially exceeds the nominal ad valorem tariff. Such discrimination and the investment distortions it produces against downstream processing by primary producers could be lessened if international negotiations should substantially reduce or eliminate tariffs on processing industries and assure importing countries, in return, access to raw materials.

An international agreement establishing ground rules for foreign investment and the operation of the multinational mining corporations could also provide certain benefits. For example, if an agreement stipulated the conditions under which a firm's properties could be expropriated and the nature of compensation, it would reduce the risk of investing in many parts of the world. This would benefit both the producers and consumers of mineral products. Those countries with high quality but undeveloped deposits of mineral products—often politically insecure countries—would find it easier to arrange the financing and technology needed to bring these deposits into production. Exploitation of higher quality deposits would benefit consumers by reducing the costs of mineral production and the prices that consumers must pay.

Many conventions covering foreign investment can be envisaged. One possibility would be to strengthen the position of mining corporations by making it more difficult for host countries to demand renegotiation of contracts once a new mine or processing facility is in operation, to increase taxes in a discriminatory manner, or to confiscate property without prompt and adequate compensation. There are today international courts for settling disputes between host governments and mining corporations, but many host governments refuse to recognize the jurisdiction of such courts over what they consider internal matters. The major importing states, however, could agree among themselves to prohibit imports from any country that violates prescribed standards in dealing with its foreign firms.[7]

Moving in the other direction, an international convention might limit or prohibit the participation of foreign equity in the mineral sectors of foreign countries. For example, mining corporations might be allowed to operate in foreign countries only through joint ventures in which they held a minority interest. Or they might be permitted majority or complete control of a project initially but be required to transfer their equity to the government over a period of time. Thus, after twenty or thirty years, the project would be completely controlled by the host country. Given the importance of near-term cash flows in the internal rate of return method and other procedures that major mining companies use to assess the desirability of mineral projects, if the phase-out period were gradual it should not greatly diminish the incentives of mining corporations to invest abroad.

Going to the extreme, an international convention could stipulate that foreign investors should hold no equity in mineral projects. The technology and know-how possessed today by the major mining corporations could be employed abroad through service contracts along the lines of the agreement that the Anaconda Company has with Iran. If the host country could not supply the necessary capital, external financing might be arranged in much the same way that it is now, under project financing. The World Bank and other international institutions would provide funds for infrastructure and possibly for the project itself. Long-term contracts could be arranged and the collection rights to those contracts sold to financial institutions around the world. The export-import banks of industrial countries wishing to promote exports of equipment needed to develop the project would also be a source of funds.

7. Such a "hot products" convention is suggested by C. Fred Bergsten and his associates, though they discourage all equity investment by nonnationals. Thus, only the rights of debt holders would be protected under their scheme. (See *American Multinationals and American Interests,* Brookings Institution, forthcoming.)

To the extent that such arrangements reduce the risk associated with new mineral projects abroad and yet at the same time do not constrain the international flow of technology, know-how, and capital, they would promote the expansion of mineral capacity. This, of course, would reduce the possibilities of shortages in the future and benefit the importing states as well as those producing states that possess the better deposits. Such arrangement should also defuse the hostility found in many countries today toward foreign investment, reducing the internal pressure for expropriation, as well as for embargoes, unilateral actions, and cartel activities.

## Policies for Depletion

All of the preceding policies focus on means for eliminating shortages, or the adverse effects of shortages, caused by inadequate investment, cyclical volatility, or artificial constraints on the international movement of mineral products. None of these policies reduce the threat of shortages that may arise in the long run, that is within a century or two, as a result of the depletion of mineral deposits. Chapter two points out that, although depletion does not pose a significant problem for at least the remainder of this century, over the longer term serious shortages could arise as a result of the cost increases of going to lower grade, more remote, and more difficult to work deposits.

Such shortages, should they eventually arise, could be quite serious. They could cause painful reductions in living standards around the world and force drastic changes in the way of life now found in industrial societies. Once the threat of depletion is widely recognized it may be too late to cope with the pending shortages with new technology and changes in life styles and family size. Some have concluded that public policy should be concerned with this potential problem today. They argue that prudence calls for some insurance against the downside risk of depletion—even though the probability of shortages arising from this source may be low or remote—simply because the consequences could be so serious. Whether the costs associated with such policies are worth the benefits is an open question. To a large extent the answer hinges on the magnitude of the cost involved, on the probabilities assigned to severe shortages arising from depletion, and on value judgments concerning the importance of future generations and the continuation of civilization as it now exists.

While this suggests that there is no way at this time to judge the correctness or to measure the desirability of public policies designed to assure that depletion does not create serious shortages, the nature of the depletion problem does give some guidance as to what types of public efforts might be pursued if public policies are to be undertaken. In particular, since technological change has been the primary force offsetting the cost-increasing effects of depletion in the past, it would appear that any public policy initiated to reduce the long-run threat of depletion should at a minimum encourage and support research and development. Moreover, since the adverse effects of depletion are far in the future and difficult to discern with precision, the emphasis should be on basic research rather than applied research and development, which focus on specific technologies for dealing with specific problems. Basic research, in contrast, concentrates on advancing basic understanding of materials and enhancing the scientific tools at society's disposal. These could later be brought to bear on specific problems as the specific effects of depletion became apparent.

Since the burden placed on technological change as mankind's weapon for coping with the cost-increasing effects of depletion will be considerably heavier if population grows rapidly, if per capita incomes rise sharply, and if a large proportion of these incomes are spent on material intensive goods, public policies for reducing the threat of depletion might also include efforts to slow population growth and to promote interest in non-material intensive activities. By reducing demand for mineral commodities, these public policies would increase the probability that technological change will continue in the future to offset the adverse effects of mineral depletion. (These observations do not override the conclusion in chapter two that depletion is not, for the foreseeable future, and may never be, a serious threat to the adequacy of mineral supplies.)

## Shortages, Public Policy, and the Future

The present investigation of the future adequacy of nonfuel minerals, although it anticipates that shortages will arise from time to time, is in many respects reassuring. It is, for example, fortunate that shortages during the remainder of this century will not be caused by the depletion of mineral deposits, for shortages induced by depletion could be long lasting, even permanent, and grow increasingly severe with time. Instead, shortages would result from problems further along in the supply chain.

First, investment in new mines and in the processing facilities needed to convert mineral ores into useful products may be insufficient. Insufficient investment is caused by, among other things, liquidity problems when markets are depressed and price controls when markets are booming. Since it typically takes two to six years to expand existing facilities or build new ones, shortages created by insufficient investment will not be felt immediately; and once their impact is apparent, several years are needed to construct the capacity needed to alleviate them.

Second, even when adequate capacity exists to satisfy demand at prevailing prices over most of the business cycle, shortages are still likely to occur during periods of particularly strong economic activity. The demand for mineral products is derived largely from their major end uses in the construction, capital equipment, transportation, and consumer durables industries. The output of these industries, and in turn the demand for minerals, expands greatly during economic booms. Since mineral supply and demand are little affected by price in the short run once full capacity is reached, shortages are likely to occur in the future during such periods. While speculation could conceivably alleviate these cyclical shortages, in the past, at least, speculation has not done so. Indeed, some evidence suggests that it has aggravated such shortages.

Third, many minerals are mined far from where they are ultimately used to make consumer and producer goods, and so at some stage of processing they enter international trade in substantial quantities. As a a result, shortages in some regions may arise because of embargoes, cartels, or other constraints on trade. Such actions stimulate the development of new capacity elsewhere, the substitution of alternative materials, and the creation of new material-saving technology, and so are unlikely to succeed over the long run. Still, for a number of reasons the possibility that mineral producing countries will attempt to follow the example set by OPEC cannot be ruled out. Cartels, even if they collapse within a few years, can in the interim create artificially high prices and shortages.

Shortages caused by inadequate investment, cyclical volatility, and constraints on trade, unlike those depletion would create, are likely to be temporary, seldom lasting more than a few years. Moreover, since they arise from the activities of men rather than the paucity of nature, they are far easier to redress. And in many cases, it appears they can even be prevented. Of the many possible policies that governments might follow in pursuit of this goal, this book considers but a few. Yet even this limited examination is encouraging, for it suggests that economic stockpiles, international commodity agreements, and international conventions covering trade and foreign investment could go a long way toward eliminating the mineral shortages that are likely to arise during the rest of this century.

In the more distant future—the twenty-first century and beyond—depletion could become a more pressing problem. It is important to stress this possibility, for the consequences to industrial societies could be most severe. At the same time, it should be noted that the arsenal available to mankind for dealing with this threat is not empty. As pointed out above, public policies that support research in minerals and reduce their consumption increase the likelihood that technological progress will continue to offset the adverse effects of depletion. Other policies, such as programs to encourage smaller families, to slow the growth of population, may be desirable for other reasons as well. Finally, even in the absence of such policies, one cannot be certain that depletion will ultimately overwhelm the cost-reducing impact of new technology. For as depletion starts to push mineral prices up, it unleashes forces that stimulate the substitution of cheaper and more abundant materials for the increasingly scarce minerals, encourages the search for new and unconventional sources of supplies, and promotes the development of more cost-reducing technologies. Conceivably, these forces could by themselves keep the specter of depletion at bay indefinitely.

# Index

# Index

109